THE LOST AMERICAN

THE LOST AMERICAN

JAMES C. PARSONS

authorHOUSE®

AuthorHouse™
1663 Liberty Drive
Bloomington, IN 47403
www.authorhouse.com
Phone: 1-800-839-8640

Published by AuthorHouse   04/02/2012

ISBN: 978-1-4685-7665-8 (sc)
ISBN: 978-1-4685-7664-1 (e)

Library of Congress Control Number: 2012906010

Any people depicted in stock imagery provided by Thinkstock are models, and such images are being used for illustrative purposes only.
Certain stock imagery © Thinkstock.

This book is printed on acid-free paper.

Because of the dynamic nature of the Internet, any web addresses or links contained in this book may have changed since publication and may no longer be valid. The views expressed in this work are solely those of the author and do not necessarily reflect the views of the publisher, and the publisher hereby disclaims any responsibility for them.

Contents

CHAPTER ONE

Courage

Where., to begin?

My story should probably be told from the very begining. So then, let me introduce myself too you and attempt to explain, if possible. some of the strange circumstances and bizzar events which have occured with-in my life and with-in the history of my very own nation. Which, has also inspired me now, to attempt to communicate with you if possible. Hopefuly sharing through written word, the story of my life and the story of our own Nations' History as a People of the United States of America and of the great importance of knowing what "camp" you are in.

As I share with you the story in-which you will hopefully enjoy at my expence.

I would like to call too mind," Freedom of Speech." and why the Founding" Fathers" of this Country would agree on the importance of freedom of speech. Being a key component with-in our society's form of goverment's operation and function. Freedom of Speech would be neccessary for the the Peoples of a newly formed Republic to post their greviences and openly debate and communicate and have a redress of complaint or affirmation of ideas. etc,. We would not be like England and subject to the Crown. but., (By The People For The People)and so on. etc.,

Today, when potential wrongs are perpetrated upon the People by, Goverment., the files are often sealed. as to protect the establishment. Why? That would definetly seem to go against the understanding of the Constitution and The Bill of Rights. what are they protecting?

Checks and Balances by the People. If we do not communicate our storys who will? Freedom of Speech is our only method as a People, to call too alarm and sound off as Paul Revere and inform the Nation of impending danger. (King George 3rd would have stopped all forms of communications if possible)

A man has to stand for something. or He will fall for anything. (So then because thou art lukewarm, and neither cold nor hot, I will spew thee out of my mouth.) Rev;3-16

Freedom of choice? How we are tested daily. exsposed to circumstances of unseen forces and measured by our ability to choose wisely. The Bible tells us ; "To be wise as serpents and harmless as doves." Mathew 10-16. still wise words.

I gave it considerable thought as to the possible ramifications of this book and God gave me time to experience the real gift of life. Which intern led me to ponder upon the frailness of man. and soon, I realized that one needs to attempt communications with others, in the effort to make all persons aware, of the Promise of Salvation.

First, as a Soldier of Christ, whom knows where he stands in the here after. and secondly as a citizen of The United States of America. with supposed rights of freedom of speech being nurtured with a freedom of the press on the side. I will now share with you my story and just take my chances with "Caesar". or "King George 3rd" and or even possibly you.

My name is . . . . and I' am probably the only "known" or more than likely "unknown" for the record, United States citizen and former National Guard member from the Beautiful State of Alabama. located in the "Bible Belt" of America. Whom, has never been discharged, never questioned, never arrested and never asked, "why?" I decided too "un-officially "resign and would merely walk away from an obligation and duty too serve as a soldier with a special forces unit from my home state. and upon returning from having recieved my training from the military establishment. I would get "lost" in America. Let me explain too you. Why, and quiet possibly How, this has unfortunately occured.

Upon returning from having recieved training as a new member of the Alabama State National Guard. I being under a sense, of distress and even fear. Not fear of foreign enemies. but, a fear of domestic enemies or" entities" instead., (Quiet possible the worst kind imagineable. no! not little green men but possibly., your very own goverment) So, I went "AWOL". Thats right! AWOL over twenty years ago and apparently no-one seems to care. (very puzzling?)

It was unbelievable! soon, after enlisting I realized that my own life was possibly placed endanger by my very own Goverment. But, who could I tell this too? A New Commanding Officer. That, I didn't even know. Or a Non-Commissioned Officer. Whom, I also had never had a conversation with. Someone. Whom, I also had just recently been re-aqauinted with They would have most assuredly thought, that I was off my "Rocker". So., I thought, I got clever and I verbally requested a "resignation" with a lie. I thought I had fabricated one of the best possible circumstances one could be dismissed for,. I had informed a Superior Non-Commisioned Officer that I had met only once before I enlisted. Whom, I also had learned to respect as a fellow special forces soldier and peer. That, I had smoked a left handed cigarette upon returning from training at a home-coming party and that I knew that I had messed up and I was prepared to take my discharge and punishment at that present time. and then he said, "Hell it's not that bad, there's a couple of soldiers around here that still smoke. It will., be alright".

But, That was not the response that I was going for., I wanted to tell someone. But, Whom would believe me. It wasn't the training. I had just completed it. ("The Human Element") He just didn't seem to understand. Why, I could want out so soon after just going through the hardest part of my training. But, I had hoped that in hind-sight he would have noticed something in my eyes and no, not "smoke". but fear and with his own inquest out of his own curiosity. He would or could seek to explain my actions, or at least wonder why? But, I was merely allowed, to just walk away. Never being pursued, never questioned why? and never having any follow ups in regard to their "newest member" who just simply vanished. and I knew why. I looked for answers and wondered and worried greatly. How long would the Goverment take, to realize their mistake and apologize and see me as friendly and not as a threat to National Security.

I saught out help through our Senate and House of Representatives. but, communication between myself and our Senators and Representatives has of yet, has not been returned. Except for on one occasion. when, One of Our Senators from my home State of Alabama called on the hard line. (telephone) and who literally wondered and asked. while, we spoke over the phone. and I quote, "What do you want me to do about it?" My reply, Investigate it! Investigate me, With my permission. What occured to me was not right. I said, In reminding Him of the content within my letter., Which was inclosed with-in my initial, correspondence to his Office earlier. Since then, I have not heard anymore, from my Senators nor Our Representatives. and yet, no outstanding warrants were ever or have ever been issued against My person. Recently, on the News just a short time ago., A story aired about a young man at one of the airports being arrested and being sent to a well known Militrary Prison for being a military deserter. While, He insisted on his innoccents and made total denial of ever having served in our countrys military services. and still, He was still detained for two weeks or more by the military Police. at least until, The Goverment finally realized their mistake. He was then released with an apology and some missing hair, I believe.

CHAPTER TWO

And then, theres me

As a youth, I had the fortune of having wonderful parents. Who, had attended Church and had given me the opportunity to be able to attend a Christian Elementary School located in the city of Gardendale, Alabama. Where, a very much appreciated education was rooted or sewn during the very first parts of my impressionable youth. In my opinion the most important time of a childs mental and psychological development. (See Brown vs. The State 1953)., I was very fortunate to having had attended the School and instead of having recieved an Indoctrination based upon the "false assumptions" of Evolutionist. I instead, recieved an "introduction" into Christianity and "Common Sense". and Our Nations rich Spiritual Heritage and some possible reasons for life it self. Which, still in itself could possibly be just merely opinion. But, it is also the opinion of our Founding for-fathers. Whom, Had established this Country and refered to it, as an act of Providence. It, too has it's own scientific merits and theories in which, some are well established and shared in fact. (Interpretations and Empirical Evidence) I have yet to see anything evolve, excluding language, clothes and a wide variety of other human inventions. Things bring forth after their kind, and have yet to be observed, evolving, and becoming a new creature. Adapting and molting. sure, But never Physicaly Evolving and changing into a New Being. "irony, that sounds like Christianity doesn't it? changing into a new being, isn't that what happens to Christians."

(Our Nations Founders were pretty smart men. They knew what it would take to insure the New American Colonies' future, with it's new form of Goverment. "By The People For The People", is the basis for Our Goverment. and in the words of Dr. Benjamin Rush, "Spirituality" must go hand in hand with education and goverment for our form of goverment to continue working properly.) an example of the of the spiritual awareness often shared in the Colonial past.

For instance Thomas Jeffersons reaction to the "Danbury letter" has been taken out of it's proper context so many times that it could be used as the so called "missing-link" of seperation of Church and State claims. There was never a "seperation "of Church and State as we are now being instructed to blindly accept as truth or at least not in the sense that has been argued so succesfully in progressive court proceedings,. The Supreme Court in 1811, in; The People vs Ruggle. ruled against a Mr. Charles Ruggle for his use of profanity. Ruling that, His "words" were a direct attack upon the Constitutions Integrity as a document acknowledging a Creator and so, The Court sentenced him "Charles Ruggle", to three months in prison and fined Him Five-Hundred Dollars and then futher stated that," He could have been sentenced for treason".

Another example of human goverment ruling on "perceptions". Five-hundred dollars in 1811, was a pretty large sum of money at the time., and not to mention the possibility of being shot are hanged until dead for treason. However, the "Supreme Court" would have to tread lightly. Since, it was also a matter of "freedom of speach" issues for the defendant.

I had attended The Tabernacle Christian School. which, is located in Gardendale, Alabama for the first two, of my twelve years of my required public schooling. but as a youth, I found myself having to move to a new town. where, I had not the "fortune" of being able to attend the same type of educational facility as before. right away, I realized that things were alot., different in Public School. The children, that is, my fellow students seemed to suffer from a general lack of self worth and personal respect for their teachers and for the school staff.

It was only later, that I realized that most of them did not really no any better as children. and like today, Parents seem to be to" disconnected" from their own childrens up-bringing and or Education., Either due to the Social and Professional stresses upon most American house holds. (The finacially and materialistic social norms, and a general dose of the dumbing down of the Society.)

Our "modern day" school system. Which is suppose to be our Public School System. Was founded on the importance of Christianity as a foundation to which the future of our Nation is to reside upon or rather desired. To ensure that the pool drawn from, during times of election, would be Insured. futhermore, That the participants were of a sound mind and aware of the importance of our Nations Christian Ideologies. The truth is, theres not suppose to be a seperation of "church and state" in the same sense that is being constantly implied by those that see the Gospel of Christ as a henderance. The Dandbury letter is! one of the most mis-quoted letters used to influence the now, dumbed downed indoctrinated masses.

Our Nations Power Houses have been dumbing down our fellow citizens for so long, too long! The letter actually clarified a question being asked my a clergy member, desiring to know, if the "Goverment" was intending to restrict the Church. and the answer was no., an infatical, No!, The Goverment had no power to regulate the Church nor the desire to do so, as in "Catholic England". Remember them? We faught England for our Nations Independence. King George's soldiers whom were predominantly Catholic "Henry the Eighth", dominated Catholic. His more oppressive form of "Imperial Catholicism".

In 2011, The Roman Catholic Pope returned to England to "re-formalize" relation with-in the two forms of Catholic Churches and most people would not know of the significance of this occurrence. But, back to the American Revolution and how all of this, quiet possibly ties in, with in my own story and just maybe, yours as well.

The" Americans" won their fight. Who being mostly Protestants according to early Census Reports were ; 97% Baptist, 1% Lutheran and 1% Catholics and 1% Other. (But the English were Catholic,) England, not easily accepting defeat. Returned to attempt to secure a foothold in the American Colonys again. Only to be defeated again, and again" ironically" with the assistance of a French pirate or privateer, in the War of 1812.

I imagine that the English Crown was pretty upset and had a Nation filled with angry veterans as before,. So, The Crown seems to have enlisted the help of a Charles Darwin. I believe, or I speculate, that a conversation must have occurred between Darwin and the Crown. If He, could accomplish their "desired goal" and beat the God believing colonials academically. It would be a huge victory for the Crown and send a "broad side" against the newly formed "Rebel States", called the United States of America. After all, Our entire premise for our Constitution was that, We were Created and Endowed with inalienable Rights by God, the Creator. Well Charles got his so called Knight-Hood, and it seems to have infected the entire United States of America within the realm or halls of academia and socially accepted norms The Legeslative Branch, the Judicial Branch and of course the Executive Branch. A real political and influential nightmare, all around. (exchanging one religious concept for another) and don't kid yourself the "Theory of Evolution" is a Religion at best. it's a matter of interpretation still.)

Now, if One states his or her "spiritual" beliefs. It's deemed, an "un-educated "opinion and does not belong in the class room, are much less in the Halls of Goverment. The Goverment has been in my opinion working against the very Peoples it was established to serve and protect for some time now. Political Parties have come and gone, only to be limited to two or three and if you are an Independent no one takes you seriously.

(Monopoly Game) Constitutional violation?

I am from the Beautiful State of Alabama like I said earlier and we or my fellow Statesmen take their Football very seriously. Sometimes to serious. While yet, most have never even attended either College. Is it Tradition or Peer Pressure? I'm still confused. Democrat or Republican? Im not a registered voter! and yet I have the gumption to speak on such matters and I'l tell you why, soon enough and you'll understand my perspective and how I can voice my opinion. and not merely cast my vote for the lesser of two "evils ".

CHAPTER THREE

UNDER COVER

One day, during my eleventh grade year. A couple of School friends asked me if, I wanted to go with them to view a couple of "paint-ball guns". At a store in Dolomite, Alabama. known as the "Bunker." Myself, being an Ambassador of Good Will. Decided, That it would be of mutual interest to at least investigate the matter futher.(Since myself and friends from my neighborhood often played "B.B' gun. War" in the woods and carelessly at that.) So, I accompanied my two High School friends to the store. With know knowledge of our destination, just the intent., and upon arrival. I noticed, That the location of the store was located along side, a familiar business (owned by my neighbor) Where, I had worked the previous summers' with my best friend. Whom, Had happened to be, the owner's son.

During our breaks at work, We would occassionaly see several employees of the "Bunker" (the store that I was now standing in front of) out side. Playing with remote controlled helicopters in their parking lot. and We, That is to say, my friend and myself would often wonder what type of store it was. But, we never inquired any futher than thought.

(When that clock moved at work and said we were through working, We left.) and now, I found myself, standing in the Parking lot of that same store, having been just invited to look at Paint-Ball guns. "huhu' and now I know, I thought." I went inside the facility and in hind-sight can remember an atmosphere of the two high school friends being more than just off the street customers. As we were allowed too, I believe, proceed futher into the establishment than someone off the street. (They turned out to be friends with the Owners)

Upon arrival and entry. We were in the store for no more than five-minutes at the most. just long enough for myself to look around and see what appeared to be assault rifles hanging on the stores' walls. Now, I am sitting down in a chair that had just been offered to me, and I'm wondering, "Are those paint-ball-guns hanging on the walls?" and, just as that thought crosses into my mind, the cow-bell hanging on the stores front entry door makes a terrible noise!

Soldiers suddenly storm through the store with rifles in hand, pistols, grenedes etc, "total combat gear and wearing no noticed insignias". At first, I thought that they were just a group of overly serious gamers and then, I noticed that their guns were real. very real and trained upon me. I was momentarily shocked, I didn't move, didn't even breathe. What was going on? am I, about too die in Dolomite? that was the thought I suddenly found myself thinking as I found myself still pretty much in a state of confusion from "shock and augh".

I couldn't help but watch one of the armed Soldiers searching through an office filing cabinet. literraly, allowing His fingers to do, the walking. I knew then, after He had by-passed so many of the Files, that they were after a Particular File. as I sat there, I guess my own natural curiosity attracted Their attention.

With a Soldier still right in front of me, searching thru the filing cabinets and Soldiers continuing clearing and securing of the rest of the premises, a man in a suit and literaly, wearing a trench coat and tie. suddenly, stepped around the corner of the wall from inside the hall where, he had been standing. Holding up Identification, indicating a well known Goverment Agency and stood directly in front of me.

He then asked me directly. "Who was I?" Being half scared out of my mind. I eagerly told the agent who I was and why I was there. and He. then, just casually proceeded to ask for my Identification.

So, I carefully reached for my wallet as a soldier stood at guard with his M-16 pointed directly toward me. All I could do was hope that the Soldiers would not shoot me. as I nervously handed the agent my drivers license.

The "agent" momentarily disappears around the wall. where, I could hear him making a copy of my Drivers license on the stores copying machine., He returned shortly after with my Drivers license still warm, from the light from the Copier and said, "We could go and that, We would be in touch". I left the store, with my friends in one of their cars which happen to have been a "chocalate colored celica" wondering, what just happened?

But, the remainder of the year was quiet. no inquiries, no follow ups. I was always expecting an un-wanted and un-needed visit from the goverment to my home and I was left to wonder, How in the world, would or could, I explain this to my Parents. But, fortunately they never came. ("Do things happen for a reason?".)

Years earlier. While, I was still attending Pittman Junior High school. I found myself sitting in my assigned lunch/study hall. With a brand new school year just begining (as a seventh grader). It was during the very first days of the new school year and the Principal of the school came into to my class room. asking for a volunteer to change classes, to be with-in fire code. He asked. But, no one would raise their hand and voulunteer. (Healthy Fear?) So, He asked again. and still, no one would voulunteer. So, after seeing the situation steadily growing more uncomfortable for everyone, I decided to voulunteer. ("just had too voulunteer")

I was moved too a new "less" crowded classroom and found myself sitting in a ninth grade lunch study/hall. right behind this Kid, who always wore this "Beret". (Little did I know then. "Coincidences?") I was assigned my desk, for the duraration of the year. and I found myself sitting directly behind the kid who would turn out to be the son of the owner of the "Bunker". (Guilt by association?)

Well, as my family seems to have a large share of "Gypsy Blood" in them. They, decided to move again. Unfortunately! During my Senior Year. So, I most unfortunately had to attend a brand new "country" High School. as an unknown student with no friends and no known past. and most unfortunate for me, was being from a "city" school. Where, student dress had a different "norm" than from the "country" setting. So I, stood out like a sore thumb. and to make things even worse. The Principal had gathered the entire High School Student Body into the cafeteria on the first day of school. and said,

"Due to the drug problems of the previous year, I had to place an under-cover Police Officer in the School "., and just like a comic scene from a strange movie,. ten heads turned and then twenty heads and then hundreds! It seemed that every face in the school was focused on me, from that moment on.

For the entire year, I was treated just like an under-cover police-officer. By the students and the teachers, alike. I was not welcomed at all. Such a terrible and strange year would un-fold; death threats, whispers in the halls, and occasionaly someone leaving small suttle signs on my motorcycle. as if, it had been tampered with on school property. Finally, the harrassment became so bad, that I had to seek help from the Schools' Guidance Counselor. When, I spoke too the Counselor and informed her of the unfolding and uncomfortable situation. The first thing or question, She seemed to only want to ask me herself was. Are you not a cop? I couldn't believe it. I told the counselor that, No! I was not a Police Officer. and Her reply then was, "OH! you do have it bad then." We spoke after the unbelief and humor of it all had subsided and She then gave me, her proffesional opinion.

So, with my High School Guidance Counselors advice. I was sent too the "Bessemer State Technical College" to take a General Educational Exam. Which, at the time was an official testing site.

I took the test and then. reluctantly returned too the High School. A couple of days later, as I was sitting in class. My name was suddenly called out over the school speaker system informing me to report too the Principals' office. So, I went too the Office, only to be met by the Principal Himself. Stating, that I had passed my General Educational Examination and that it wasn't fare too the tax-payers for me to remain in the public school system and also, I had successfuly graduated before the rest of my Senior class.

So, I held my head up high and walked out of BrookWood High School.

CHAPTER FOUR

LITTLE DID I KNOW

After leaving the High School in Brookwood, Alabama. I decided upon making a career as an United States Soldier in the U.S. Army. ("little did I know") I went too the United States Army Recruiters' office in Bessemer, Alabama and layed it all upon the table. I told them all that I desired and all., that I was willing to try.

The Recruiter listened intently and arranged for me to take the Military's Entrance Exam. I took the Test with about sixty other possible inductee's and waited patiently for my test results. While waiting, I began to notice that out of all of the applicants whom had also taken the test. My group was some how left waiting, forever, on Our results. The other two persons whom had ridden with myself and the Recruiter were growing very impatient. As we were now, the last group waiting on our test results.

The Army Recruiter kept making trips back and forth, back and forth between the Building where the testing had occured and the recruiter's car. Where, myself and the other two applicants were now, all three impatiently waiting. The time of the Delay? was ridiculous and even the Army Recruiter was growing indifferent. We just patiently kept waitng and talking between ourselves, about the stories you hear, about the military always making you wait.

Finally, after the Recruiter's last trip into the testing site. ("and upon returning to the car, The recruiter sat in the car and gave me the stangest look. I didn't think too much about it at the time, I had not connected the dots as of yet.") we were then driven back too the Recruiter's Office. Where she said, that she will talk with everyone else first and then, she would speak with me. So, I went out side for a breath of fresh air for a short period of time and then, was invited back inside too speak with the U.S. Army Recruiter. After, she had finished speaking with the other two.

The Recruiter asked me again, about my desires within the military. again, I found myself repeating my objectives. I wanted too serve twenty years are more, go to College, and possibly become an Officer and serve within the Special Forces arena if possible.

The Recruiter looks at me. and says, "Even though you had made higher than most persons taking the test, they had to grade you on the "curve", and thats what took your group so long." I asked, What Curve? The U.S. Army Recruiter said., Because, I have a General Educational Diploma, I was not qualified for any Branch of Service. except for the Army., possibly as a Cook or even a Truck Driver and because of my "G.E.D."., I was not qualified to recieve any G.I. Bill, Benefits. and then, all of a sudden, a First Sergeant whom had apparently been listening in, from His office. from across the hall. Stood in the doorway of his subordinate officer who just told me something strange.

Standing there with the years of service on His sleeve and the Honors awarded. are more or less earned on his chest. and stating. That, He had never heard of anything like what had just been said to me, before. (Everything that I had said must have impressed upon Him because He futher stated), You sound like the ideal candidate for the Special Forces. and, that He, Did not know why His subordinate was telling me what he and myself had heard.

("Hind-sight is worth so much, if we can only see".) Well, the Sergeant proceeds to tell the "First Sergeant", (Higher ranking Sergeant) that He (First Sergeant), didn't want any part of the matter. and then, The First-Sergeant looked so confused. and I have to admit, That I myself was a little bewildered.

"Why was this lower ranking Sergeant speaking to their superior First Sergeant in this manner. Were they friends? Was all of this some "set up" like talking to used car salesmen?" (dishonesty implied)

I wondered., But the First Sergeant was slightly more confused at the circumstances apparently unfolding. and as for myself, I had not connected those dots. I decided to listen to the Higher Ranking Member and was told that, He didn't quiet understand what was going on and that I should literally go speak with someone else. ("I probably ruined that mans career".)

I decided to follow His advice, as He advised me of the 20th Special Forces Group, attached too the Alabama National Guard. The National Guard was not what I wanted. But, He informed me. that once in, the" Federal Goverment" might just purchase my contract from the State of Alabama and I would be able to easily switch too active duty then.

Well that certainly sounded better than the National Guard. So, off I go to the Recruiter's office on Oporto-Madrid. I walked in and introduced myself, and found myself in augh, as I found myself speaking to a real life Green-Beret. I attempted to hold myself in the most proffessional and respectful manner as possible as I spoke with the Recruiter who was most receptive and proffessional, and the only thing He could ask was. Why did I pencil in a new score on my test? (refering to the A.S.V.A.B)

I enformed the Recruiter, that I had not altered my paperwork or test score and that the Federal Army Recruiter had done that, or at least she said the testers had done so. His reply, We don't do that! ("get out now Chris") was what I wished someone would have said. But no one did. The Special Forces Recruiter stated that there was nothing wrong with my test scores and that they had an opening, if, I was serious and maybe just maybe the Federal Goverment would indeed, purchase my contract. Once I got in and showed them what I could actually do. But, because of my G.E.D., I wasn't qualified to recieve any college benefits. and, Once again, He, was confused as to why, I was not eligable to recieve college benefits. (I was just seventeen and kicked out of High School for a G.E.D.)

Sounded better than a cook, sounded better than a truck driver, Im not knocking those professions, I just had alot of gumption at the time and wanted to be all that I could be. So, I enlisted during late October of 1986. at the under ripe age of seventeen.

(Be All You Can Be) what a slogan.

CHAPTER FIVE

Basic Training

I arrived at Ft. Jackson, South Carolina. After a long bus ride. I finally found myself falling into a sloppy formation of new recruits, just outside of a Barracks or building., that was obviously going to be our new home away from home. As we displayed our civilian and personel items, so publicly for the entire world too see. We, that is to say, my new set of friends, and myself became aquainted with the atmosphere of the military order.

We stood in formation, nervously opening our suit-cases and spreading it's entire contents upon the ground, around our feet. left at attention. We anxietously awaited our own personal meeting with our own" personal" Drill Instructors. as They, slowly walked thru the formation adjusting everyone's civilian mind too a new form of military mind and life and as you know it from now on, introduction or welcoming speach. Surely given too all new recruits on their first day. or, at least that was the way I recieved it. (no problem)

Training began with the basic standard introduction into the required military "attitude adjustment." Recieving the basics of being a soldier, How to eat, How too shower, how to shave and how to keep your weapon clean. You exercised daily and recieved general military combat and leadership training., You either performed profesionaly or sub-standerdly and you did not want to do the later. You did that, and you recieved correction. stiff correction! embarrassment, physical punishment of course and intimidation. But, I didn't have that problem. I seemed to fit right in. A natural born soldier. (oh' the irony.)

Like I said, I seemed too fit right in. I guess, being from a family where I had a set of parents whom one had been an active member

within the United States Navy, and one whom is a real "neat freek ",
and both parents being very well structured within the disciplines of
hygiene, cleanliness' and the respect of the chain of command and of
course an up-bringing that was goverened by such established principals
had in fact, prepared me for military life.

Both parents with very good heads upon their shoulders, had seemed
to have prepared me for an easy transition from civilian life too military
life.

Drill-Instructors would size everyone up as a whole and then,
probably as an Individual. I'm not really sure. where, I would "place"
within their assements. I like to think that I was the best one that they
had. But, one can never know, what one, is thinking. "see polygraph
machine", an inside joke for you that I will elaborate upon later,.

My Drill Sergeants were very capable Instructors and I already
had a healthy respect for their position and profesions. I listened and
followed instruction. as, it was instruction based on years of accumilated
knowledge that was aquired thru blood and sweat. But mostly, Blood. I
knew why and what they were there for. I had watched the war movies
growing up (Sergeant York and Audie Murphy, and All Quiet on the
Western Front) They were not there, to be sadistic or cruel for their own
pleasure. They were there to teach me and my fellow soldiers, the basics
of military life and too form us, with the "cookie-cutter approach".
mentality and physically molding us into a soldier. I respected them
greatly, and after the first couple of weeks, I believe after being sized up
and tested repeatedly, I must have shown both of my assigned Instructors
that I was squared away. So it seemed, as if we were actually becoming
more like friends, rather than just Instructor /Trainee.

Training was full filling, enjoyable and very exciting. I seemed to fit
right in. I was a quick learner and a motivated young soldier. and then
one day, the trouble began. Not much at first, but, very important just
the same and then the beginning of a very strange relationship between
myself and my goverment began to un-fold.

A question of my academic achievements or requirements was in
question and not by my Instuctors whom had been training me. But,
by two plain clothed goverment employees. Whom, had approached me
during one day after training. To inform me, That because of my lack
of a high school diploma or a "General Educational Diploma." I, was
going to have to aquire one. If, I wanted to stay in the Army? and I

knew right away, that there was a huge mistake. I attempted to inform the two "G-men". That, I had in fact recieved one. after all., It had gotten me kicked out of High School. It was supposedly used to reduce my "ASVAB" score., and now, They are saying that I do not, even have one., hu? (It's My Document. I think I would know that I have one)

The gentlemen began to inform me that I could recieve toutoring along with a handfull of other recruits. whom, also were to aquire their "G.E.D.s," after each days, training activities. But, I wasn't going to. I did not need to. I again, tried to tell the gentlemen that I had. in fact, recieved one. while, I was still in High School and that this was obviously some sort of mistake. But, the Gentlemen continued to insist that I would have to obtain one. So, I wrote home and requested a copy of my document to be sent to my address as soon as possible and I patiently and eargerly awaited for the mail.

Training continued daily as usual but not so usual as anticipated. While, in my fox hole, on the top of the firing mound at the firing or rifle range, with my assigned buddy beside me. A shot rang out! an "un-authorized" shot rang out! Sand suddenly explodes up into my eyes! Was it me, I momentarly thought to myself. "darn". I was almost shot! no more than a foot away a single rifle round strikes the ground. Right there, striking the ground just in front of me so close it almost killed me. Who was it? was it me? I admit, that was my reaction, because it happened so close too close.

We were at the firing range as usual recieving training just as we had done the previous day, before. No one, No one was suppose to have any live rounds Having" live bullets" when you were not suppose to, was a bad thing! Do they know it wasn't me? I stood there for a moment in confusion having to convince myself that it wasn't me that just fired the shot. But, the sound, the sand, it was so confusing to me. So, myself and my buddy checked on each other to see if each other was alright and both of us were a little excited to say the least. Im sure. We stood their nervously watching and awaiting as two Drill Instuctors marched across the top of the firing burm into our general direction, in a slightly hurried up rate of speed.

I'm still wondering, Do they know who did it? Do they know that it was not me. As They began to get closer and closer, I started to think of the consequences of the event. I almost, died and they, were probably going to kick me! out of the Army. Because, They want know that it was not me. Simply, because it happened so close. Well, They, the two Drill-Instructors came right too us., that is to say, my buddy and myself. But, fortunately for us, just one fox-hole over., Both of them, at the same time, reaching down., grabbed some soldier up under his arm pits and snatched him up and literally dragged him down the entire length of the firing burm, backwards., the entire time with his boot heels plowing into the top of the ground, with this dumbfounded are even shocked look upon his face! and a face that we as a platoon never saw again. Instead, I believe He may have been recycled or even discharged from the Military. I'm not really sure of this recruits fate.

CHAPTER SIX

THE HUMAN ELEMENT

Training as usual. I guess, "it always seemed to be the other guy". My Drill Instructors and myself seemed to have developed a friendship. While, I was under their military authority.

They would show me usually once and I would reciprocate on command. I never had any real difficulty adjusting to military protocal or lifestyle nor delay in learning. I was always willing and excited to perform and show what I could actually do. I like to believe that I had earned my Drill Sergeants respect and appreciation of having an honest desire to serve my Country. (Real Gung-Ho) As, I recieved training as any other recruit. I constantly suffered harrassment from other Drill Instructors. Whom now, in hind-sight, One could easily assume that they had been orderd to single me out. (Since, they were not "my" Drill Instructors)

One day, During Basic Training. I had approached an amo bunker. Where, I was sent to recieve my allotted rifle rounds from another Drill-Instructor. and as I was standing in line with everyone else. All, "chaos" suddenly broke out. Right there. literally, just at my feet! As a Drill-Instuctor had approached me with the "devil "in her eyes! A fellow Drill-Instructor from a running position. literally, tackled the Drill-Sergeant and both Sergeants were then rolling around violently at my feet. They proceeded to fight with each other with more intensity than you can possibly imagine., rolling back and forth, back and forth, practicing or utilizing their combat training on each other. I just stood there in shock with everyone else. What in the world was going on? Where, am I? This place is a madd house and They, are suppose to be our trainers? or, at least that question is certainly legitimate in regard to at least a couple of them. and then, all of a sudden. Another Drill-Sergeant must have seen everything that had just happened and came running over and restored some since of order. or maybe just assisted the restraining Drill-Sergeant from doing what they may all have wanted to do?

I was never quiet sure. I was right in the center again. why? I don't know. I' m actually a pretty observant person. I constantly watch people, not because I mock or belittle or berate them, but to learn and observe from my fellow human beings. So, Healthy Human relations can be established and knowledge passed on. (We All have the same Ancestors)

So I, have watched a whole lot of people growing up in my life and never have I noticed this sort of "wild behavior" before. Being, displayed or directed at or recieved by anybody other than me or even the "week link "in the platoon. But, That was not me. I was the best Soldier out of the entire platoon, and my Drill-Sergeants, I' m sure, would' agree. I would Help the weak link in my platoon, because I knew that they wanted too serve their Nation as much as I wanted. (not too mention, keeping my platoon from being unnecessarily punished.) the "Ambassador of Good Will that I am."

During another average day, during training. a Drill-Instructor whom again was not my own. but, still assigned to the Company. asked me. if I, was Central Intelligence? I admit, I was a little confused. Why, in the World would this man, a Drill-Sergeant be asking me this question. At that time, I had still know idea' and had not connected the dots as of yet. I answered the Drill-Instuctor with I'm sure, a typical response. "No! Drill-Sergeant." He just stood there. and seemingly accepting my response He just casually walked away.

I continued on with my training as everyone else. I had made alot of friends and really enjoyed the atmosphere within the military just the same. even with all the insanity around me. There were those moments that out-weighed all the strange occurences. and I, ignorantly still hoped for recongnition of my abilities and hoped for positive reports. which, I had assumed were written in all forms with-in the proper military channels. Which, I had still hoped for establishing and warranting a change in my military contractual agreement between the State of Alabama and the Federal Goverment.

Training continued as usual, or as" they" the days were expected and had been planned out daily by the U.S. Military and at the same time General Educational Classes were being offered. But, I wasn't going. Not out of disrespect mind you. But, anger and principal. If I had attended the classes when those around me had not had to present their own Diplomas. Why should I? There was a precedent to be aware of in creating "acceptance". That I could allow myself to be treated differently "Academically" from my fellow soldiers. after all, I had already earned my G.E.D. in "Public School ".

Day by day training became more and more exciting and I never knew exactly. where, I stood. or what crazy event would present itself for the day., and I was now, nervously awaiting for the mail. which, had hopefully contained the transcript that had gotten me kicked out of High School and was the same, used as an excuse to lower my A.S.V.A.B. score by the Military Recruiter.

Chapter Seven

SUPER BOWL

"Super Bowl", or thats what the Military called it. It was a testing phase toward the end of basic training. When, all that the recruits had learned had to be displayed, on command. All that they, or I, had learned during Basic Training. Drill Sergeants would apply pressure upon the recruits to see if we actually retained or could perform under pressure and demonstrate what we should have learned within the time that we had shared with-in the military Institution and with it's respected Instructors during Our Basic Training. So the Company was broken down into it's respected platoons and we as a Company marched for several miles again, and finally arriving at a pre-arranged testing field.

We as platoons were then broken down futher into" sticks" (small groups) we would then move out into the field in set intervals to ingage different task and situations relative to the duties and functions of a modern day foot soldier.

While testing with the {light anti-armored weapon}., I was placed under the direct Supervision of the Firing Range Officer on or in that particular testing site. Whom, happened to control all activity and in-activity at His "assigned" location. We were ordered into position as a line of "Napolean Soldiers" or Colonial maybe more appropriate.

We stood at attention and waited upon command before we moved, being very attentive and proffesional. The Firing Range Officer would engage each soldier one at a time and commit to testing each soldier on the knowledge and know how of the weapons system. It soon became my turn and I was well trained and prepared for the testing to begin. So, upon recieving a direct command under the Firing Range Officer. I was ordered to display all knowledge and practice of the "laws rocket".

I displayed my ability with the weapon system successfully and professionaly, too the satisfaction of the Firing Range Officer. and upon completion, the Firing Range-Officer gave me a "pass" sign. and then proceeded to give me another direct order too proceed too the next testing site. I then, noticed that while I would be carring out his direct orders. I would also be, theoretically placing my self in danger by walking directly behind the other soldiers whom, were standing there with deadly weapons in their hands.

Since, He was the only tester on site. I enquired with the most profesional inquery into His exact specification with-in his order. asking, if, He was just testing me again in regard to the dangers of "back-blast". He just smiled at me. and said, "No. get out of here, You passed Soldier!"

So, I proceeded to carry out His direct order. When all of a sudden, a Drill-Sergeant who had been facing the other direction. apparently, instinct or being a nervous reaction. Suddenly turned around to karate chop me in the chest. But, I also being a martial artist, found myself in a very uncomfortable position. Should, I just let this man just hit me or do I retaliate. No! I could not do that. I would have been kicked out for sure and thrown into jail. So young and dumb, I pivited and snapped to attention, and created a fulcrum point with my upper arm. resulting in lessening His blow. The Drill Instructor then jumped "in" my face and stood there, eye balling me. I could sense him debating with-in himself if I had just did, what he "probably" thought I had done. and just as he was about to chew me a new rear end., I was suddenly rescued to my surprise by The Firing Range Officer whom had just tested me moments earlier. and apparently had just observed the action. I didn't complain as He (The Firing Range Officer)came to my aid. Not, that I had asked, But just because it was the right thing to do, I guess. It's what I would have probably done. I stood there at attention, listening to the Firing Range Officer chewing the most unfortunate Drill-Sergeant a new butt, instead. It lasted for several minutes actually, and I was begining to feel actually quiet sort of "sorry" for the Drill-Sergeant. and then, I thought of the under-table retalliation that I was probably going to recieve, and that made me very nervous. and I hadn't even had done anything to justify theDrill-Instructors potential assault. The Firing Range Officer re-issued his order and I carried it out. and moved on to another task and another site.

Later in the day, at chow time. I found myself sitting down with my buddys and we were just preparing to eat our meals. and then Suddenly, over the loud speaker an announcement was made and I found myself being called to report to the Senior Drill-Sergeants Table. I was more nervous than ever before. Why, was I getting called to the "Senior Drill Sergeants" Table? Was I, in trouble? Did I, do something wrong? No! I will just do what I am called too do, and report in.

I, like a little boy, reported in. To then, what seemed like the table of the Great Elders.

Nervously I reported in and found myself wondering within myself did I even choose the correct words to sound military enough as I approached their table. The table just sat there motionless as I spoke and the Senior Drill Instructor just sat there. Kind of reminding me of a charactcer from one of those war movies, that I was so familiar with as a child.

His very character demanded, no warranted respect. He was a true profesional soldier. and He, just sat there. and began speaking of a situation that had just been brought to His attention in regard to an assault which had occured upon my person. I just stood there thinking, crapp. Who said something? It was not me. I had the thought suddenly, how all of this made me look like a" complainer" and I had taken everything that they kept throwing at me! Not once have I complained. and now, Here I am, in a very uncomfortable and new situation that once again, I did not create.

The Senior Drill Instructor stated that it was brought too his attention that I was assaulted by "Drill Sergeant H".(thats what I will call him to save his face, although he knows who he is.") I was assaulted and the assault was reported by the Firing Range Officer and I could. or, at least he, the Senior Instructor wanted to know. if I, wanted to press charges against the Drill-Sergeant and destroy the mans career quiet possibly? There it was, I had not even complained. and It was not me that had said anything to anyone. It was the Firing Range Officer after all. But here it was, making me sound like a slacker, a complainer, a little boy who wanted to go home and bake some cookies with his mommy., ("That was the phrase or wording often used by the Instructors when they thought of someone with an attitude problem"). and (I do like to Bake Cookies with my Mom. Morones!) just a recent thought.

I instead, simply told the Senior Drill Instructor that there was no need for disciplinary action. and that It was an unfortunate mistake on his part and I held no gruge against the Drill-Sergeant and futhermore, I stated that, I would not want to ruin the mans career and throw away all the years of service. because of an infraction or misunderstanding on his part. The Senior Drill Sergeant just sat there at the head of his table, listening to what I had to say and then, just smiled. and said. Good, the problem is resolved then, carry on Private.

I noticed my own Drill-Sergeants sitting at the table and they just seemed to smile as well as with acceptance or maybe pride in my proffesionalism, seeing that they had been the ones training me? or the other side of the coin would know that they had not trained me too be a person of good character and take it so lightly. (Whats in a smile)

And still, training continues. The following days went on with little or no un-needed harassment or adjustment from any military staff members. Until one day when all of a sudden the two plain-clothed "G-men" approached me again, In regard to my academic standing within the famous, "Educational Halls of Academia" and the requirements or the standards to be met of the United States Armed Services and I, had just also had recieved my much awaited letter from home in regard to my General Educational Diploma, just a day or so sooner. and I was eagerly awaiting on their futher enquiries into my "academic standards" so, that I could proudly present my Diploma and put their minds too rest.

I was told by the "Gentlemen" earlier that I had to take the test. pass it or find myself getting booted out of the service. So I proudly presented my documentaion to the gentlemen who seemed to instead debate whether or not it was good enough? They replied, "You will, have to get your General Educational Diploma". (the same G.E.D., that got me kicked out of High School? The same, said "G.E.D." that was used to justify the "reason" for lowering my A.S.V.A.B. score. The same G.E.D. that has caused me so much trouble?) The same G.E.D. that the Two G-Men just recieved from me and whisked away. Yep. I felt like an arrogant fool. I should have been studying with those other soldiers. whom were cramming for the test for weeks. But, I refused. I was sure that all of this would have been cleared up. But nope, grab a seat and sit down.

I took the test and found myself always finishing every part before everyone else. Was I being over confident again? God I hope not. But, that was all I could keep thinking with every portion of the test administered to me, being completed. So I would wisely spend the moments reviewing my work. The test was finished up after about three or so, hours and we were released back to our individual Company's and platoons later that night.

The following day was training as normal, nothing really notable just more of the same. And a couple of days later, as we were suppose to battle with the batons demonstrating the using of ones rifle and bayonet. Where, I would have been meeting with the Drill-Sergeant whom had assaulted me earlier. Possibly due to the fact that he turned out to be the Martial Arts Instructor or due to the fact that I would be attending Airborne School after Basic Training, I apparently, was kept from attending that particular exercise, by having to suddenly obtain an Airborne Physical. Due to my individual advanced training course of service. "It was probably a good thing in hind-sight, to quite possibly have someone arrange for that, to have occured". I was sent by myself to take this much needed harder physical for Airborne School after hopefully graduating Basic Training. But, as things were, I never really knew where I stood. I passed the test or met the required physical requirements for Airborne School and continued on with my instruction in Basic Training.(seeing that I had to be administered the test for Airborne school even before I had succesfully passed Basic Training,)

CHAPTER EIGHT

AN EDUCATION

A forced twenty mile field march with packs was standard practice at the time and During the course of training. The Company had to participate in a tatical forced march, with-in the accepted time. It was a very interesting exercise to have paticipated in. With an entire Battalion being moved by boot and the human will.

Upon completion of our march as a Battalion, My Company Commander ordered every platoon to fall into a horseshoe formation in front of his Head-Quarters, and then the Captain addressed the platoons one by one and then my platoon was called to the Captains' position. Where, The Captain gave a speach about the importance of an education. He, seemed to just go on and on, for at least thirty-minutes or so. It became a very intimidating and lengthy speach and then finally, he said., There were over "five-hundred or so" new recruits on the base that had to recieve their "G.E.D's" and Out of all, of these. unfortunately! were only a handful. They were just required to take this test just a couple of days ago. The Captain continued to express the importance of an education and the importance as an United States Soldier of obtaining a proper education and the severe consequences of not. He continued on and on, in regard to the importance of an education. and then I started wondereing whether or not, I had just possibly been drumed out of the United States Military.

The Captain continued speaking to the dismay that he had felt and that he would notify you if you had failed the test. However stating instead, it would take too long to read all the names of those that had failed to recieve their General Educational Diplomas and it would be easier to just read the names of those soldiers that had instead, passed.

He continued, dragging out his remarks, leaving me growing more and more concerned, and then finally, after a very lengthy point of time. Stating the importance of an education one more time. Finally said, out of all of these soldiers that know, whom they are, Their were only seven that have passed. "Im more nervous now, than ever", and then, He proceeded to read out loud, the names. "and I' am thinking what are my chances?", after all, I decided not to attend the toutoring classes at night and then here I am. The Captain started reading the names out loud and all of a sudden I heard my name called out around the fifth person being referred too., I momentarily felt a since of relief and then, embarrassment. I after all, had not dropped out of High School, I was kicked out of High School for that very same General Educational Diploma. and now, I just received another one and had to suffer all of my friends thinking of me as a High School Drop out!, Right away, with good intentions. My fellow soldiers started complimenting me and began patting me upon my back. (But I hadn't dropped out!)

Well, after being almost shot, being double gassed for no reason in all honesty, and assaulted by a Drill-Sergeant, and Targeted by other Drill-Sergeants and Had been denied all "Academic "professionalism by the very same goverment who created the desired standards for the American Educational System to begin with.

I was then congratulated and then bragged upon. By my own Drill Sergeants and then, used as a topic of motivation. as, The Drill Sergeants gave us a "fare the well speach" after completing Basic Training. and noted' that I was the only Special Forces designated "M.O.S" out of the entire platoon and then, as my Drill Instructors actually spoke adrressing the entire platoon as well, I then really noticed for the first time. really, that they themselves were Airborne. I didn't know why I hadn't noticed before, maybe because that was my new destination.

CHAPTER NINE

IN THE DEAD OF NIGHT

My arrival at Fort Benning in the dead of night. I arrived at the base sometime around mid-night with two other airborne students. Upon arrival we were told that we were either two weeks early or two weeks late," typical army fashion, hurry up and wait. Continuing to check in or reporting in for duty, I was futher informed that, I was required to take an Airborne Physical. because, apparently I had not been administered one. I began to attempt to clarify that situation with a calm demeanor, and communicating to my recieving School Administrator that I had just taken one at Basic Training just a couple days prior. But, they just re-stated that I did not seem to have one on file and that I would have to pass one again and someone would be around eventually to "administer" one to me once again. hu,? The other two persons that I had just reported in with didn't have to obtain anothr pyshical and one of them was a beautiful girl and the other was smaller in stature than myself.

We were assigned to a different set of barracks for housing and kept seperated from the current classes. But we still had to fall into formation with the current Airborne classes at every formation. I and some new friends were pretty much cut loose everyday and given free reign to stomp around the base. except for times when I and the other two, whom I had happened to report in with, were given kitchen patrol or even instructed to literally police up the base. (and for those of you not familiar with the military, it simply means to work in the kitchen or pick up trash on the ground.) I passed the first couple of weeks, waiting on classes to begin and then on the weekends, I was let loose to do as I apparently, pleased. During one of these weekends two Non-Commissioned Officers aproached me late in the evening and made a comment on my lack of after hours activities and that I should accompany them to the Bases' pub and have a couple of drinks. I was very intimidated to do such a thing. since after all, I was just out of Basic Training and experiences with Sergeants had not been that favorable. But after some convincing on their part, I reluctantly and nervously accompanied them and soon found myself being bought and brought drink after drink, after drink. There I was, a "private" in the Alabama National Guard, and all I wanted to be was regular army and now, here I am drunk! I decided that this after all was not probably in my best interest, so I got up and left. I went straight back to my barracks and laid my head down for no more than an hour. But it seemed like only minutes. when all of a sudden, with a loud bang! Two Sergeant Airbornes or "black hats" (that was what we were to refer to them as), woke me up violently! To inform me that I had to take an Airborne physical and it was either pass or fail, no second chances! ("and if I didn't pass Airborne Training I was washed out, due to the sort of M.O.S. that I was assigned. ") Still a little drunk I pushed on, and began around three o'-clock in the morning. I had no choice in the matter, I couldn't just re-scheldule and get back with them. So under great pressure and strain, I gave it my all and succesfully completed the testing. Probably aided more by my own anger! I passed the strenuous exam and began training the very same morning. I fell into the formation with Sergeants, Officers and alike and some from other Branches of the Armed Services all together. I felt slightly intimidated, Who was I? Just a Little Private, training side by side with Captains and Majors and Non-Commisioned Officers of every rank, could I do it?

CHAPTER TEN

HEIL MICKEY!

The very first day of training I observed that all ranks were being treated just the same., you made a mistake no matter what your rank was and you recieved swift and stern punishment only the "Black Hats" ruled there. I was personally assigned to probably the largest man I have ever seen in my entire life. Every morning the entire Company would have to give a large "Heil Mickey" greeting in cadence, and soon I realized that the Instructor or Black Hat had taken a special interest in me for no apparent reason, He literaly seemed to have searched for me in particular and you did not want that! you never wanted to be singled out for anything and I had just arrived I did not even have time to have messed up, but none the less, I was singled out and intimidated as best as possible.

The "Black Hat" had a clear fondness for the Looney Tunes Cartoons apparently and quickly associated me with "Elmer Fudd". He would even go so far as "attempting" to get me to impersonate the cartoon character when ever he needed amusement, quiet possibly or perhaps it was a meer tool to assess my mental strengths and weaknesses, perhaps,

Training proceeded with no real problems, I mean you do what they do, you do what they say do, how they do it and it seemed pretty straight foward. We ran everywhere, We ran to school which consisted mostly of sand pits, where we exercised and exercised some more, and then we learned how to fall! over and over again, I was very much enjoying the moments, after three weeks of constant running and sit ups and push ups and jumping jacks and learning how to control ones body upon departure from a moving airplane, We finally moved to the air strip and suited up for our first of five required jumps, as I waddled toward the air plane, loaded down with gear, extremely excited! one could say because, I had never even flown before, and all I could think of was, How beautiful the plane actually was, and I was finally going to get to fly and jump., But I was not scared, I trusted in the training and those that had trained me, after all they were not in the buisness of hurting their on fellow Americans, even with all the, at times sadistic behaviors on there part, it would reflect upon them and they just wanted us to do it right and be able to operate under pressure, Well thats what I told myself, and I trusted and still trust in the GOD of CREATION, So I being one of the youngest in my stick was given the opportunity to be the first one out the door.

I stood there as trained, watching the terrain passing by. Reminding me of a little nativity scene or a scale-modelers interpretation of a beautiful country vision. The jump light turned green and away I went. With out any hesitation, relying upon my training and my constant belief in God, I jumped out of the plane without any fear. instead, a sence of peace and tranquility took over. (maybe because at that moment you are as close to the Creator as possible) As I seemed to just float through the air, I looked up and checked my canopy to make sure it was deployed, looking around for hazards and checking my rate of descent. I looked for my fellow soldiers in the air and nervously awaited for the fast approaching ground,. I then sized up my position or falling position and pulled the appropriate parachute risers into my chest as hard as one could. Suddenly, I hit the ground as hard as a ton of bricks. But, I just rolled right out of it, as trained. I momentarily layed there on the ground acknowledging what I just did. and then, I proceeded to roll up my parachute and run out of the drop zone. We went straight back to the air strip and recieved a newly packed parachute and were made ready to do it again. Four more jumps to go! can I do it with out breaking a leg or foot or worse, loosing my life?

CHAPTER ELEVEN

JUMP MASTER

C-130's, are very beautiful airplanes, I wished that I had been given the opportunity to be a pilot instead. But, there I am. Four more jumps too go, and then I am officially Airborne. My second jump went without any event. I jumped and floated through the air like a baloon. I went through the same procedures as before, relying upon the training that I had recieved; check your canopy and descent speed, check for traffic and decide which landing position would best be suited for your position relative to the ground and wind direction. Really a controlled human crash landing if you will.

I rolled up my parachute again and then ran off the field, always looking above for falling soldiers out of the sky! I proceeded to the airfield to make my final jump. I recieved my new parachute from the Airborne Rigger and suited up or dawned the parachute. I then borded the plane and flew over the drop zone anticipating the very last jump and what was this story of "blood wings" all about, that is, if I made it.

I did not always have to stand in the door as in the begining., maybe, they realized that I instead would not hesitate after all. They tell everyone, that they will place the youngest in the door first, in an attempt to inspire those other airborne recruits are volunteers to be well motivated to jump and not freeze in the door. Maybe, they did. it really did not matter after all.

The Jump Master opened the door and stood in the opening. looking out, He had spotted the drop zone. He then gave the command and the stick stood up and then hooked up on command. A soldier moved to the door with the rest of his stick and froze in the door.

Why? then, I don't know. Maybe they were having problems with him before, I m not sure.

The Jump master whom only had a monkey harness on, proceeded to motivate the soldier to exit the plane. But, It didn't go well for him at all. He got the soldier out through the door but . . . , the soldier wasn't going to go out that easy! He, literally grabbed hold of the Jump Master and pulled him out with him! (Planes are a terribly noisey enviroment and no person can actually communicate verbaly due to the noise when the doors are opened so hand signals are utilized to relay commands.) I' m sitting their in the plane directly across from the know on going activity. Wondering to myself, How it must have felt to be pulled out of a flying airplane at an altittude of fifteen-hundred feet. All of this time, four awesome jumps under my belt and now this. I was in shock actually. It seemed sureal, did I just see what I think I saw? I continued sitting there with my eyes steadily fixed upon the door and then it caught my attention. The Jump Master was on the outside of the plane with only that little strap holding him or keeping him alive! I wanted to do something but I couldn't. Theres a reason that seems logical for the Jump Master not to be wearing a parachute. It would have been very dangerous for someone to start actually working and risking a premature parachute opening within the airplane., It could really place everyone on board in danger and even possibly bring the airplane down. I just sat their motionless as I watched a real soldier get pulled right back into a flying airplane. Straightening His goggles upon re-entry, and then checking his harness, (his life-line)and just kept right on working like nothing even ever happened. I bet every Airborne Soldier had a new found respect for that man at the door. I wanted to say something but no one could hear you. I just handed the man my static-line and jumped on command.

CHAPTER TWELVE

JERONIMO

Falling with grace, not from grace, I exited the door with a loud "Jeronimo", for the first time but no one could hear me, and I let my training take over, I gently floated through the sky watching for fellow soldiers on possible collision courses and observing the fast approaching ground, I did it before, it does hurt a bit, and yet sometimes or at least on one occasion, I could have landed on an egg without breaking it. I saw it coming, Here it comes!, like a ton of bricks I crashed upon the ground and then I realized why we spent so much time running and practicing falling, I got up and rolled up my parachute, jaming it into the drop bag, and throwing it across my back I ran off the drop zone as fast as I could to the pre-arranged meeting site. I dropped off my parachute and was informed to file into ranks as we arrived in groups of ten at least and no more, where we stood at attention, being greeted and congratulated by now our fellow Airborne Soldiers whom had been our Airborne Instructors just hours earlier. We stood there as Airborne Soldiers as they shook our hands, pinned a set of airborne jump wings onto our chest, without placing the safety catches upon the backs. We as a group new what was to come next as the Officer placed the un-pinned wings on your uniform, He would skake your hand and then proceeded to the guy beside you, His assistant would come behind him and slam, the wings into your chest as hard as he could, literaly pinning them to your chest, "blood wings". I don't think anybody that I had trained with, had any problem with the tradition of recieving blood wings. We actually helped the system along as we each congratulated each other, Officers and Enlisted alike re-slamming each others wings into their chest! The more blood the better, after all, we were a little gung-ho.

We all recieved our newly appreciated status, as airborne soldiers and the removal of the former status as "leggs", with much pride and reward, and were assigned to our new postings, as for me, I was on my way too Fort. Lee, Virginia to under go my Advanced Individual Training as an Airborne Rigger. I arrived at the base and soon realized that we, that is, The Airborne Soldiers were far and few between on the entire base. I would fall into formation within a new company of soldiers just out of basic training, Whom were probably wondering why were they there with these special forces soldiers. Had the military messed up there orders somehow? I can only speculate and often do, it seems to be a plague upon my being now. "constant speculation".

CHAPTER THIRTEEN

SUPERIOR RAGE
Training at Fort Lee.

Training was a little different than I had originally thought that it would be, I believe because my platoon was the only airborne platoon on the entire base, although there were probably more, we or I just never saw any. The Senior Drill Instructors assigned to my barracks were more of a friend than one to intimidate, maybe because he too was Airborne and knew that for the most part, We were more squared away, at least more than those Soldiers just out of Basic Training. I continued on with my training meeting alot of very interesting people, The training that I was recieving was broken down into three seperate Training Schools. Where, I had the fortune of training side by side with Navy Seal's and Marine Recon and a couple of Airforce Para Rescue and Foward Combat Controllers. The Marines were not always causing problems, but some times with their indoctrinated superior egoes they can make it hard to work with and actually thats how the Marine Corp is I believe, They prefer to work alone due to the realities of their function as our History has displayed time and time again. and then however the Navy Seal's were a bunch of guys that I really enjoyed training with. I actually found myself recieving the very same training as Marine Corp Recon and Navy Seals and yet, remember I was told by my Recruiter that I wasn't capable academically to do so or at least based upon the alterred A.S.V.A.B., test. Which was supposedly changed because I had a G.E.D. and not your standard Diploma. "Irony" rather insult! or What?

During training, while training with the United States Marine Corp Recon, I developed a friend-ship with a Marine who seemed to know why we were there training together with the Country's other special forces groups and of the importance of our team work., and yet everyday when his superior would see him cooperating as we were all commanded to do He and a couple of the others, would constantly find himself getting chewed out by their Lance Corporal. and we, would all have to listen to this "superior rage ". About, how much better they were than everyone else., and I would just stand there in dis-belief as ones ego would interfere with training and suggest such an undesirable attitude. (Who will turn it off?) Day by day, it was the same thing. My admiration for the Navy Seal's grew stronger and my opinion of the Marine Recon did not change in the slightest. and then, on a very strange afternoon an extremely beautiful Marine Corp "female" reporter came by. To do an in depth story on the Marine recon, whom were recieving their training in "union" with the other military units. However, the reporter seemed to pay more attention to me. Why? I don't know. it's not like I'm "photo genic". She begins or proceeds to take several pictures and then interviews a couple of the soldiers and then after a short time. she just seemed too disappear, and then, a couple of days later, as I was re-viewing notes upon a table with a Navy friend, My Marine Corp friend flops down a Marine Corp Gazzet, "with me, right there on the cover". A huge cover shot, and then my friend started laughing, and He stated that his Lance Corporal was "upset". and said to have asked ; How could this have happened? "I seemed to look more like a Marine than the Marines "and those were his words". I just stood there, not realizing that I was on the cover of the United States Marine Corp Gazzete.

Test day, after having finished ones Advanced Individual Training you again, had to display what I or you had learned. For me it was being an AirborneRigger, which meant preparing repairing and packing your own parachute, packing and preparing multiple cargo parachutes for cargo air drops and. I would have hated to have failed. "I just thought of that". Well I proceeded too the airfield and boarded the airplane again and then jumped out. and then as I stood slightly off to the side of the drop zone a "C-130" flew over carrying my cargo. I stood there in relative safety on the side of the drop zone, Awaiting the plane to release my cargo over the field and one after another the cargo boxes were pushed from the airplane and they just kept coming out., there was a total of at least ten cargo bundels to be dropped and one by one the cargo-chutes deployed and slowly opened, except one, it just instead, seemed to have had its wind stolen from the number of cargo-chutes and it instead shot through the sky like a blazzing meteor with the parachute material trailing violently behind. No fire, but what a sight all the same. This gigantic box approximately six by six by four foot tall, just shot through the sky with my name all . . . , over it. It slammed into the ground like a meteor from the classic scienc fiction movie "Attack of the Worlds" and I, went to go look for the potential problem. and upon arrival I became very impressed at how deep a wooden cargo box, full of junk could really penetrate the earth. I proceeded to do my job and visual attempt to acces the potential problem visually only. Since we were not allowed to touch the packages until they were tested for any human errors and I didn't see anything wrong, the package should have been slowed down by a deployed cargo-parachute., but it wasn't, I was a little upset since the seriousness of the matter and my overall grade depended on a successful operation. Later, I would recieve word that my cargo drop under review, was complete and then I would find out if it was my fault or not. My Instructors returned a "verdict" and ruled that the evidence showed, that the tight grouping of the drop resulted in a cargo parachute having it's wind deprived or stolen by the other parachutes. I get too graduate, not really much of a ceromony, just another set of wings and a congratulations from someone you didn't even remember ever meeting. My entire class recieved their orders within the first week of the completion of their training and shipped out, but not me.

CHAPTER FOURTEEN

LIMBO

"Stuck in limbo, are what would become my very own twilight zone."

At Fort Lee Virginia, I just remembered that several of the soldiers that I had the fortune of being trained with would later be sent too, Mogadishu Africa. and un-fortunately would participate in what later would come to be known by the Hollywwod Movie," Blackhawk Down"., but, as for me I was stuck in Virginia, oh the irony, there I was, All I wanted to be was "regular" or "federal" Army. From day one, serve twenty years, and then go too college and hopefully retire from active duty and then pursue other career oportunity's with the United States Goverment. and now, an Alabama National Guard soldier whom, had just finished his training and knew where He was suppose to be unfortunately going. But it seemed as someone else apparently didn't. Everyday, I would fall into formation with an entirely new class and then fall out on command as they prepared to march off to school. Everyday for weeks and then months. Still, with no orders and no offical results recieved in regard to my official request into changing my status., I had just assumed that it had been relayed by my own recruiters' office and then my Basic Training Instructors and everyone that I had communicated with so far.

So, I watched new classes come and go, come and go," I believe". and by that, I mean I really don't know, for sure since some of my memory appears or seems to be absent or a little "hazy" if you will. and I will elaborate later. (although) "I have been giving the system a chance to come clean. But now, protest and complaint being made with no response and correction, I have weighed the consequences of my possible actions and have considered the frailty of my mortal life and have concluded that by penalty of death or imprisonment this story must be told."

I would fall into formation with a new Company for a period of time and then, as classes would prepare to march off to school I would be dismissed from the formation to carry own.

I would find myself hanging out with the Company's Senior Drill Sergeant. Occassionaly playing a game of pool or watching the daily news and occasionally runing an errand or two and being allowed to walk to the Administrative Offices'. Where, my orders were to originate from., I had also developed another friendship with a very attractive military administrative clerk, whom would always do her best to find my orders during the many visits that I had made too her office. But they never seemed to arrive or manifest themselves.

During one of these days in limbo I was called for to report too a Colonels office. Why? I don't know, it was certainly out of the peramiter of the social norm. I arrived at the address that I was called to and I can remember placing my hand on the door handle to this office and then right away, I found myself sitting in the most comfortable chair I have ever sat in. A huge chair which in hind sight seems totally out of place, it was an orange colored chair that seemed larger than most standard issued pieces of military furniture.

A Colonel just sat behind his desk as a Major seemed to be kneeling beside me. I never, never, forget a face! But, I never remembered theirs or even why I was there in this office in the first place. I can remember hearing the Colonel telling the Major this. and I quote, "He doesn't know anything", and then, I don't even remember leaving the office, the next thing I experienced, I find myself standing in a phone booth, just outside of my barracks when I came to. as if, I had come down with the walking flu or evena case of amnesia. I could not remember how, I got there or even how long, I had been gone. I suddenly felt the need to grabb hold of the phone booth and then realized that I had the reciever in my hand. I was confused! I instinctly said, helo' helo'., but their was no one on the line. I hung up the phone and operating in a state of dizziness. I reached into the coin slot for change out of habit, and found no change in the machine. I nervously walked out of the booth and started heading in the direction of my barracks and suddenly the thought that I was absent without ordered leave, or, a.w.o.l. took over me and I couldn't explain it! Where, had I been? I nervously walked up the sidewalk back toward my barracks wondering how much trouble was I going to be in? and looking into the windows for a familiar face, I realized that I didn't know anyone there anymore, there were no familiar faces. They were all new! and as I approached, the Senior Drill Instructor whom was assigned to that station, suddenly slung open, both doors upon my approach toward the front of the Barracks. It was during the middle of the afternoon when I arrived and all of the soldiers were in the schools and with a larger than life smile on his face, the Drill-Sergeant stated that my orders had finally been cut. "convenient timing," and still in a fuzy daze or a sense of "what just happened"

I cannot remember preparing my possessions for departure. I guess I packed and as I was walking toward the bus stop still in a daze I recieved actually kind words and pats on the back, in the Army? really! I boarded the bus and got back to the State of Alabama somehow. (What Happened?)

I reported in to my unit upon returning from training and recieved orders to participate in joint training exercises in the Beautiful State of Montana. I was to accompany a fellow Airborne/Rigger. Whom he, and I, would be the only two Airborne Riggers for the entire operation., We arrived at an old, dilapidated base in the afternoon and began to set up shop. But, due to the weather turning unfavorable for parachute operations, we sat., For two weeks. It seemed to be just a beer fest. I would find myself in the small bases' pub, as it was used as an "un-official" meeting area. Green Berets, Pilots and Officers alike, all drinking and relaxing and then it dawned on me! I do not even know these soldiers and they do not know me, or do they? What was going on? It would be easy to get killed. I became suddenly afraid. not afraid of the enemy, nor afraid of falling too my death under the right circumstances, like war! But, afraid of them, the system! It was immoral and corrupt. I realized my life was in danger, and there was no one that I could confide in or trust. So upon returning back home to my State. I decided to lie to my superior controller and tell him something, What? I didn't know, I thought about what would be believable and what would not. I knew, if I told them or him the truth that they wouldn't have believed me. So I lied. I told the supervisor that I had been smoking pot or marajuana and that I felt that it wasn't safe for anyone to take a chance on trusting my ability to prepare parachutes. (I wasn't proud of that lie, because I hadn't smoked any pot, it just seemed at the time the best legitimate reason for being discharged.) I didn't know the man personally. but, I had met him before I had en-listed into the service and upon returning from my training within the army, I noticed a small section on the wall containing notes and communication in regard to my training. They were actually keeping up with my performance and progress. and now, I m telling this man a lie. I think he saw right through my lie and attempted to difuse the situation by telling me that it was going to be alright. but, I was dead set on keeping up the front. Again, I insisted that it wasn't in his interest nor our fellow soldiers for the chance to be taken. and then, I hoped that he could see the struggle in my eyes.(I was under a form of duress and I couldn't express what had been hapening). So, he just looked me in the eyes and told me that I never had to return. and being young and dumb and scared out of my mind, I didn't return, and however, I didn't go into hiding. although I tried checking out of society for a while, unsuccessfully at that. As the years rolled by, I had time to reflect on the past events and realized that the problem was bigger than I could handle alone, Who would believe me? and should I allow my Constitutional Rights in which we, all live by, be denied. Making me a criminal by{ in-active }representation of the fact or facts in question. It would set a terrible precedent allowing ones nation too deny the peoples' rights. baring in mind the nature of ones goverment. (Republic for which it Stands)etc.

CHAPTER FIFTEEN

HALF CITIZEN AND I DON'T KNOW WHAT ELSE

And so this is the part of my story. where, I wished I had never found myself. and, its all true and I am willing, to share it with you.

Because, I know that it will help you learn why and how, I lean toward my way of thinking, too some degree'. and if your still willing to read. I'm still willing to tell. But, I will tell you this. Im not an "angel" I am a" sinner" and I have certainly done more than my share, of" bad deeds". So indulge me a little and let me tell you all that has transpired to the best of my ability.

I became seriously confused for a long period of time. and I wasn't quiet sure what to make of it all. I had attempted to pick my self up from that strange occurence(by my boot straps as they say,) and I would take some form of civilian employment and work on" re-adjusting "too my new suroundings and I found myself only questioning my "State of Citizenship" and of course, private life as well, or what exsisted based on my status and relation with my own goverment. Very sad and confusing to say the least so I began sinking deeper and deeper into a state of depression. and I knew what had happened to me was not right.

Every where I went, I became continuosly reminded of my peculiar situation. My Parents didn't know anything. and it would be possible if they had just thought of me as a slacker. Due primarily to the nature of the un-believable "odds" that seemed to constantly surround me. I was suppose to be in the Army. it would seem now, "Blindly" serving my Country.

My life started falling futher and futher apart. I had no one to confide in. Jobs would come and go, or I would. and I have probably worked for more buisnesess than anyone. Like from a movie I saw once "I have a set of skills etc.," that have served me well.

(I've never voted.?) I, being just seventeen years of age. Enlisted into the United States Military while President Ronald Reagan was the President and Commander in Chief. and He, was a Republican. and I was a soldier not too concerned with my nations politics. indeed, serving blindly.

What Political Party then represented me? I wrote too one of my State Senators and shared with him everything, as best as I could that had transpired while, I was in the Army. and even while, I was in the Public School system. See'ing how some of the possible "points" in my situation were connected directly with my academic standings. or at least that was the initial pretense for the different career oportunitys being "re-defined" toward my person at the "military's" recruiter's office. I've written letters hoping for an advocate. and am I just suppose to trust the "military's lawyer's,"? after all, it was the system itself or the other "Parties" of some other agency that railroaded me. (Who could it be?)

My State Senator's office actually suprised me and telephoned my parents house., Fortunatelly for me, while they were away. (What's He done know?)and the Senator responded to my letter and had responded "himself". and proceeded to tell me, that He had personally recieved my letter and wasn't quiet sure what I thought He was suppose to do. I expected as much. It's a strange story to believe. I was sure that I had made it more than clear what had occurred and that as a citizen with inalienable rights I had deserved better! So I responded to the Senator and communicated my complaint again, verbalaly and politely over the telephone. but, the Senator just politely left me with a "What do you want be to do about it?" I responded with, Investigate it at least, with my permission Investigate it. Still I recieved no assistance nor recieved any futher communications from those that are suppose to represent.

I guess, its just alot for anyone person to comprehend or attempt to correct. So, I decided the best "advocate" for myself was of course, myself. I then decided that I would attend College and study the law.

(with the mis-guided notion that since I was never discharged there would never be a report of the conversation between myself and the last person I saw in the military and I had never presented or was asked too present, any evidence or proof too support my verbal statement. merely word of mouth and private conversation at that. nothing official.)

So, I enrolled into a Local State college. where, I would begin too proffessionaly study the law with the hope of getting my "train", back on the tracks and since, I truly had a desire to catch the bad guy, "we need a bigger net by the way". I was your straight "A" student. dedicated too the pursuit of the aquisition of an understanding into the crininal mind and human psychology and an excitement for forensic sciences. College wasn't as hard as my High School teachers had said it would be and they do from time too time, hand feed you the information. (maybe because your paying them for their time or possibly your just ready and now more willing to learn.) knowledge is power!

I would have these conversations with my legal proffesor and Instructors from time too time in a friendly and strictly "Academic" sense.

The Second Admendment clearly states that we have the right to "keep and bare arms"., and I would find myself bebating in a healthy manner my personal views and understandings of our Constitution and then the Proffesor would speak on behalf of the system of goverment that we all share. and the college instructor would take the stance that law Enforcement Officers would carry their firearms clearly exposed. (Healthy Fear! Polocy) While, I would argue that the citizen must violate the Bill of Rights by concealing their own fire arm. and I clearly voiced my opinion in regard to the "consequences" of the" Healthy Fear Policy". and stated and re-iterated the {Bill OF RIGHTS } and why, this" Healthy Fear Policy" was bad for the Nation. and I would attempt to explain it like this.," If the people are afraid of their goverment it is tyranny and If the goverment is afraid of the people, it's a Republic.

And thus. "We The People of The United States of America". and then I would speak in regard to our elected officials and the duty of our Congress and their Constitutional allegiance and if they displeased their constituents they are removed from office or voted out. He just looked at his straight "A" student, stopped the class and asked me to accompany him too His office. "I'm thinking O'h no! I just got into trouble at school. I've never gotten into trouble at school." I nervously entered into his office a lttle confused and a little stumped. as to why? was I being isolated. and then the very first thing he actually does is to take the "anarchist-cook book" off the shelf., and handing it to me. directly, stating. "That very viewpoint is the first thing that "anarchist" have suggested for years. I just stood there, and a little insulted. Did he just call me an anarchist?. merely, because I"m knowledgeful of the Constitution and the Bill of Rights I think he actually did. Well that would figure then. He will be "educating" or rather dumbing down Society's Children on behalf of the Goverment for years to come, I'm sure.

I however continued to make straight "A"s' in his classroom. and I had considered, that he too like myself may enjoy a healthy debate from time too time. So, I would continue through college studying criminal psychology and forensic science awaiting my graduation. and then, I realized that I would never be allowed to obtain the position as Police-Officer., much less, make it through the ranks to become an Investigator. Even though my college record and training would reflect the ideal qualifications. It became or was derived through a very slow and prolonged series of painfull episodes with-in the mutiple Police Agency's around through out the State. I was never going to be hired. I had taken the "Civil Service Exam" at least seven times I believe, or more. I have even directed others into the methods and actions for applying., I had become an un-official expert on applying and taking the test. but, never hired. I went through every loop that one could jump through to no prevail. I once even learned that I could get direct sponsorship from a potential employer too attend the Law enforcement Academy. So, I applied for the position of Jailer /Dispatcher for my local town. and I was hired and welcomed by the officers on the payroll. I was on the job for more about one week and a day. I had three prisoners in the jail already directly under my supervision and the police officers in the field were depending upon me to work the computer system. Which, is a very valuable asset for any Police Department. I was an acceptional jailer/ dispatcher and suddenly I was terminated without cause by the Mayor. whom, had just apparently returned from a National Town Mayors meeting conducted during the Clinton Administration.

The Police Chief was just sitting at his desk when the Mayor returned. and then, the Mayor walked right pass my office and straight into the Police Chiefs office and told the Chief that I could not work there.

The Police Chief was totally confused. So he replied too the Mayor, and informed him. that, I had been there all week with prisoners in the jail and that all the Police-Officers liked me and that I was the best that they had ever had. but the Mayor wouldn't listen or maybe He just listened to someone else? The Police Chief re-stated his point of view. From clearly, a more knowledge-ful perspective and was instead. directly! threatened with loosing His job.

The Police Chief, then gets up from his desk and walks across the hall too my office and says, I'm pretty sure that you have over heard our conversation and that I don't know why you are being let go." So he and myself walked over too the Town Clerks' Office. where, He had my only pay check as a Dispatcher/Jailer written and then in dismay apologized on behalf of himself and the town. (another job loss that would be labeled as my own fault, by those that are being victimized with in their own Country.) "Oh' the Stepford Citizens".

CHAPTER SIXTEEN

INTERNAL AFFAIRS

Broken but not destoyed, is it true that, what doesn't kill you only makes you stronger?

Im not much of a quitter without a fight. But sometimes you need to quit while the quitting is good. never feeling completely derailed when I should have been I sought out every avenue possible. I would obtain what at the time seemed like another dead end job, until I was hopefully hired by a Police Agency. (Blindly desiring to serve still) I worked in the Furniture Buisness for a while, and then in the" Home Construction Field" as a wood carrier and then finally as a skilled carpenter., a Truck Driver or Logistics Specialist and as a Security Guard armed and unarmed post. and a dozen other proffessions., from the Docks on the water too the Docks in the Gutter. From the Mines too the Blinds. and no pun intended, I have worked for a window treatment company as well. (just to mention a few) and learning from these proffesions, that one could and would use later in life. was actualy not a bad thing after all. I eventualy realized that I had learned a great deal in Life. and there is still so much more to learn in life. However, It wasn't necessary a bad thing after all. Sure, I have had more jobs than you could shake a stick at. But, I can guarantee you that I have aquired alot more real life knowledge and experience than most working those same single jobs. and in our world that tranlates into either Goods or Services and being well associated with both of those needs, I became more Independent in that I have developed a deeper understanding of the dynamics of our materialistic life styles. primarily, career and home-ownership. Which, allows me in my opinion to see things from a different perspective. For instance, I have aquired thru the course of my employment "History" the skills and under-standings of Home construction and the finacial expenditures' one will encounter in the constructing of a new home and that, in it self, has become knowledge or economic power. which also contributes too the housing problem and the economic task that lay before us today. But that should be a different book. ie. the housing problems we are currently experiencing. (Whats in a dwelling?)

So After taking the Civil Service exam for the last and final time. and passing it, as before. To my surprise! I finally, found myself being invited to take the next step in the hiring process. A physical and an additional written test and then the ever popular polygraph test., after taking the written test and passing it. I was then invited to stay and take a "P.T." test and upon a successfull completion, I would then be invited to participate in the "commy detector test." ("foot note, if you think that a machine dreamed up, by the writer or creator of "wonder woman" can really tell you if someone is lying too you, it may be too late for you.") I then eagerly took the polygraph test knowing that it was the last test standing between myself and a carrer at last and then after being administered the test I was oddly told that the last question in regard to "communism", had given me some problems. Some problems?

(That would make me the first "Bible Believing Christian Communist" in the entire World. I thought. I'm not a communist. I am a Christian first and then I am a Constitutionalist! Thank You! but what a crock of crapp!)

Is a pattern imerging?

However., after taking the "polygraph exam". I was then instructed to proceed return to the first floor and have my picture taken for my Academy Identification. I m going to the Academy was what I thought. I was definetly placed under the impression that I was finally going to be able to attend the academy and finally, be hired.

I met with the Officer in charge of the Academy's Identification services and proceeded to have my picture taken. As with most of the senior members that I kept meeting, They all had something in common. oddly enough, my cousin whom, I had not been named after., but through strange coincidence we had shared the same birth name. and He turned out to be the person that had played a part in the hiring of some of them twenty or so years earlier. and my name stuck in their minds and due to the similarity I would find myself engaging in friendly conversation at their insistance. I couldn't lie and tell them that we were not relatives nor could I reciprocate their feelings in regard to the man. So I would always just politely explain my distance to the person they thought so fondly of. and present myself as the candidate they were testing. (That sounded political didn't it? but true just the same.)

(I have never "ridin" anyones coat tales and I was not about to start.), I would explain that he was a relative. But, I really did not know him personally. none the less, they were for the most part understanding. on face value at least, but under the table?

Three days later to my surprise I recieved a letter from the "Greater City" Police Department. indicating, that I had turned them down and that they were really looking foward to me being an employee for the "Greater City". I imediately called the number on the letter, and informed the officer that I had been looking foward to this oportunity for some time and I also., stated that I had attended college to become a better than average Officer and I had, Not! turned them down. However, I was told that I had unfortunately missed the academy start date. "Im just recieving the letter Tuesday, and I had just taken the polygraph exam Friday., and now, I am being told that I have missed the Academy start date? on Monday. I replied, "What did I miss, Orientation?" The Officer are whom ever it was on the other side of the phone restated their message and continued to inform me that because of the mix up, I would have to run through the entire process again. Well, it only usually takes over a year! So politely thanked the officer and I hung up the phone and reached for the phone book instead. and I decided to look up the number for the "Internal Affairs Office" and was able to speak directly with an internal affairs officer., The Internal Affairs Officer, was quiet receptive over the phone and asked me, if I, still had the letter. I replied, "yes sir, I do," and He then proceeded to instruct me to send Him the letter. I with-out thinking are questioning of their integrity agreed to send them the letter and He(The Officer) said that he would get back in touch with me as soon as He found something out. It wasn't long at all around three days or so, He finally did actually call., and stated; "James, its Our Local Police Department Letter Head. They are police department phone numbers. But, I don't know who it was that has sent you this letter. (It would be funny, if it wasn't real.)

Later, I even called upon the State Troopers Office requesting your general generic information in regard to applications. The office put me on hold for a period of time, approximately ten minutes or so. finally returning to the phone, an Offical, began to ask me a series of common sounding questions, age, residency and of course height. I responded to all questions and then upon telling them, that I was five-foot and eleven inches in height, I was immediately told. that I was too short. too short? (is that not discrimination or conspiracy?) I replied.," well then, Thank you then anyway", and I hung up the phone. What do you do remain silent are sing like a bird from the Highest tree of freedom.

Never being the one, whom gave up so easy, I kept knocking on the doors, I knew, that if I really wanted to clear my name, I would have to continue working to advance my cause. and later at that' would I find my "cause".

CHAPTER SEVENTEEN

ARE YOU C.I.A.?

Not out of it yet, I heard about a sort of around about approach that I might be able to utilize. "The" Local "County Deputy Sheriffs Reserve Department." I filled out an application, and with-in a couple of months, I was notified by the Department that I would have to be interviewed and pass your standard back ground investigation. I eagery agreed and the process was set into motion. and I passed? I guess what was a half "done" investigation and proceeded to meet with a panel of my peers, Whom sat, on a panel like a scene from the last supper. as you sat in front of the panel of peers answering a wide variety of questions and displaying self restraint while being pressed upon. with questions attempting to measure your mental capacitys or facultys if you will.

I'm not sure if all prospective applicants recieved the same line of questioning that I did Since, I wasn't priveleged to sit in through the entire screening process. I held myself in a cool and professional manner and seemingly passed. and I was sworn in and then issued a Badge and Commission Card. I was assigned to the Forestdale region of the County. Where, I would be assisting other Law Enforcement Officers and patroling the district as a Volunteer Officer. with the opportunity to also attend the first local deputy sheriff's law enforcement Academy. I would patroll every month and attended the Academy every assigned or required class.

While on duty one night with my assigned partner I noticed that our patrol car was being followed from the rear., and that the tailing car had in its front seat an actual proffesional grade camera system trained directly upon our squad car. (that was being driven by an officer whom, I had not known or had met before that time.) Right away, I told my partner that he had better make sure that his tie was on straight and that he had better make sure our car was dead center in our lane. Because there was a car behind our's filming us., The first thing my partner said in response, to my statement was, "What are you paranoid?" I thought how strange., "I assumed that most people would have responded with, where?., but not him, He just slowy turned his head and looked at me and then said, what, are you paranoid? and we continued on. later with-in a couple of weeks or so. While, I was reporting in for duty in the down town "Greater City ". I found myself just out side of the Main Office having a cigarette with a fellow superior local County Sheriffs Deputy. It was a beautiful day and the conversation had opened with and then right out of the blue, "Are you C.I.A.?" The man literaly asked me if, I was C.I.A.? I believe in hindsight that he must have probably recognized the confusion and or disgust upon my face. But, before I could respond, He told me to forget it. He then futher stated., He didn't know why he had even asked that question. and then, He attempted too suggest that sometimes he just had the bad habit of thinking out loud.

Sure, I had heard that before. it seems as though, even the system itself isn't sure who I work for. a couple of weeks later or less, I was called into the Chief of the Reserves' Office, along with two other Deputies. as we walked into the general meeting room we were suddenly informed that the U.S. Attorney Generals Office, being operated during the Clinton Presidency had potentially viewed all Reserves as an armed group of thugs likened unto the "militia members." (and we all remember Waco, Texas.) So the Chief continued on inform-ing us of this unfolding situation, and that we could stay and take our chances or we could resign, and He would understand if we chose the later. without delay, I reflected upon my own quiet rememberable experiences with the Federal Goverment and quickly decided to resign from my position.

CHAPTER EIGHTEEN

BIG BROTHER

The local State College has an aviation program. and I had attended the College before studying Criminal/Justice and reluctantly I decided that I may need to change my entire line of thinking all together. So I made a journey to the school to aquire the desired enrollment information or application for the general aviation degree program. I've always wanted to be a pilot. I proceeded too the School and was notified by the staff on site that the aviation Instructors were at the schools airfield. which was really just a small private airfield shared by the school and the local community. also being located on a different side of town so I drove toward the airfield and upon arrival, I found myself being so close to the mode of transportaion that I have always been so fasinated with as a child, the airplane. Excited to say the least I introduced myself too a couple of the instructors as a potential new pilot and they were very welcoming and quiet sociable. I suddenly found myself having a very interesting and very shocking conversation where I had recieved the most interesting news.

A "foreign "person had brought an expensive helicopter to the School to recieve training. and a flight instructor from the College whom had thought that He himself was checked out on the air-craft, took to the sky with his "student", and almost killing themselves and spectators on the ground, apparently had a very hard landing and a damaged the aircraft. The Helicopter or aircraft was just left sitting at the School's private airfield for six months or more. before the Aviation Administration came out and confiscated the air-craft.

Upon hearing of this report I was amazed and puzzled but not detoured in the slightest. I was still set on attending aviation school so

I was sent to the Main Campus to aquire a student official enrollment application into the Aviation Degree Program. and while., I was there, The Chief Flight Instructor asked his general school enrollment questions of me. and I had asked my questions of him. During our conversation I had noticed that a "Mini-Bell Helicopter" was sitting in his class-room bay. Intrigued, I asked if I could see the small aircraft as we were continuing to have an on-going conversation. When, Through the course of our conversation He soon had discovered that I had never been awarded or even granted benefits under the G.I. Bill. and questioned whether I had used all of the funding. since, I had mentioned that I was a Criminal/ Justice student before my inquiry into the program. I proceeded to converse with the Head Instructor and recieved the Schools Academic Packet. With" information packet" in hand, I left the school returning too my home only to notice in the reflection of my storm door, as I was just about to enter., a silent running capable Helicopter, no more than a hundred feet away and twenty feet off the ground, hovering in my next door neighbors front yard. and just hovering there and seemingly to just watc wanting to watch me very closely. I just slowly turned around in disbelief with "What in the World?" in my thought and I decided to just wave and suddenly the the Helicopter that had so stealthily descended, ascended into the air and slowly flew away. being left with wonderous amazement and excitement "what was that" I continued to open the door and walk into the house. and In less than two-weeks," Terrorist" flew our planes into our buildings killing thousands on 9-1-1. Who? then is the Goverment watching. still in doubt?

CHAPTER NINETEEN

IT'S PERSONAL

During all of these events that would be considered "professional" there is another side, the personal. Before, I began studying the law, I had fallen in love, with a wonderful girl at the time. or so, I thought. The first time I had laid my eyes upon her, I was strangely struck with that little poison arrow. We were serious for several years. She had a child from a previous marriage and Her little child grew or at least I'm sure, grew up thinking that I was Their biological father. I had wished that I was, but unfortunately I was not. and still, everyday, and I mean everyday, I would ask my "longated" finance' too marry me. but, every day her reply was the same. "we cannot afford it!," My job and her job didn't seem to ever be enough for her. But, every so often I would demise some new cleaver way of asking for Her hand in marriage. but every time I asked, I would always recieve the same answer. "No! We can't afford it!" So I tried every trick in the book if their was one written? Im sure I did it. but never a positive yes! always, "we can't afford it!" I even took Her to meet some of my less fortunate friends, whom hadn't alot of money, didn't have an exspensive house, didn't even have good health. just to show Her that if they can be married, theres' no sound reason why we couldn't be married.

However., like so many women in America, she was indoctrinated to seek the "material" first and then she might find love. But this is a foolish mentality based entirely on the premise of earthly possesions bringing fullfill-ment. which they do not. (They are distractions)

So one day, My "prolonged" or longated fiance' decided that she needed a new car. Because, hers was getting a little to old for the long commute back and forth to work. So, after five-long years, and mind you constant denials. I reluctantly, agreed to purchase her a re-conditioned car. So, off we went toward one of the many, car dealerships in the "Greater" Birmingham area' and as we arrived at a dealership, one of many. we parked the car and got out and started walking hand in hand through the car lot., we approached the cross roads suddenly or the metephorical "T", as it were. The used cars were on the right side of the lot and the brand new cars were on the left. Suddenly! I felt her pull hard towards the left, and pulled hard, She did. I instinctively assumed that she just wanted to just look. So I walked with her again hand in hand through the car lot. She(my fiance') then walks staight too the most exspensive car on the lot and a gas guzzler at that, and gives me a choice. I could purchase this car for her or she was leaving! Well., I was a little thrown back! How could this girl. Whom, had been saying for the last five-years. We can not afford to get married! Had now, some how, come to the conclusion that I was going to purchase her a fifty-thousand dollar car. and she, was even an "educated" girl. I told Her that I couldn't do that. but, I was willing to purchase her a more reasonably priced automobile.

But still, she refused., and then stated that she was going to leave. if I, didn't buy her that car! and the very next day she left. "coincidences". A couple of years later, when my human emotional wounds had healed, I found myself falling in love again. just when, I had sworn off all chances of a having a normal life I suddenly and unsuspectingly met a most beautiful young lady. She was so wonderful, I thought that all., of the past experiences were just that. they were Gods training missions (or they were distractions of the devil, Im still not very sure.)

We started dating and within six-months or so I felt passionately moved to ask for her hand in marriage. and she accepted! Wow, she accepted! I was so happy I could just see our little children right then in my minds eye. (yes, I have been a romantic), "and no. I do not ask every girl to marry me"

We or rather She planned a wedding in the summer and all of the details were being tedeously worked out. and that's when, I started realizing that the ceremonie was considerably more exspensive than I had desired. and I adressed the issue with my future Parent in-laws and conversed with them that I knew thay loved their daughter greatly and yes traditionaly, the Brides Parents have carried the burden of the cost and that wasn't neccessary. I loved their daughter very much! But a hundred thousand dollar wedding was a little crazy. and then., I was told. Don't worry about it. We are loaded! We have so much money, your kids will never have to work a day in their lives. (I went into shock! no way.)

I did not propose to their daughter because of her money or their money. I hadn't really been the type to chase after rainbows. and of course most people have said that I too often keep my head in the clouds and I should come back down to planet earth, because of my beliefs in the Almighty. but come on? The girl I was with earlier . . . , was a gold digger. but not me! (What are the Odds?)

CHAPTER TWENTY

COINCIDENCE

Meeting the relatives, "are their coincidences?" as, I was getting to know all of the family members in my new to-be family, I was informed on one afternoon that a couple of my new couisins were coming over too my future in-laws to meet me. They had heard that there was going to be a wedding. and they were only doing their part as relatives. However, I never was really was one for putting on the show and my "confidence level" was not really up to par at the time. So, I was a little nervous., What if they don't like me? What if I do or say something stupid? Will I start to studder, I never have before. but you never know.

My hands were getting sweaty as I kept finding myself asking if they were here yet? are they here yet? I asked again and again., You would have thought that I was the girl. yea, thats funny. A car then pulls into the driveway as I am standing in my future Parent in laws house. and then the door bell rings. and to my surprise and I'm sure someone else's as well. It turns out to be my ex-girlfriends, the" Gold Digger's" best friend. and, Her new Husband and there little child. The same girl whom my ex and her-self had decided earlier to take a poll of me in regard to now. But at the time, Her possible future husband. Well, there we were, all just standing there. They knew, I knew, but did my fiance' know? It was a pretty nervous moment and afternoon, to say the least. How many girls actually tell there best friends. why, they actually dumped there boy-friends. Did this potential couisin-inlaw think the worst of me? probably. That seems to be the way my luck are karma flows at times are just sits there in a stagnate pool. (So much for Evolution)

Suprisingly! the wedding plans continued. no arguements are wild accusations leveled and the wedding plans to my surprise delivered a very beautiful wedding ceromony.(in hind-sight it was probably because of the money that had already been spent.) So we were married and went upon our honeymoon., We returned in safety and moved into our very own place. with our future shared in common, We were married for an entire month. before, I was tricked into getting the marriage annuled. In one day, I went from being the best thing in Her life to becoming an un-wanted nightmare! and I had treated her as a princess, and would have gladly moved moutains for her if I could. or, if She would have only truly loved me. Since then, I have sworn off all relationships and resemblence of a "stepford life." The years left me bitter and angry with the social norm. What is wrong with people? I tried to do everything everybodys way, but I have come to believe that it is not in the cards. and Casino's always have the favorable odds, and I do not want to play anymore. (Pun)

CHAPTER TWENTY-ONE

A RECAP

Polotics, would you also believe me. if, I told you. That I have not, even registered too vote. I mentioned it earlier but would you be surprised? or would you say. Well! no Wonder! It's People like you that have let this Country get so bad. By Not Voting! And Then I would Say, Boy You Don't Know The System and the Supreme Court Decisions that have steered this Nation down the wrong Judicial Path of Legal Precedents before I was born.

The Supreme Court Judges are "political party" appointments to the established Supreme Court Bench. and voting for President has been reduced into "choosing The Lesser of The Two Evils". When You vote, what do you hope for? A President Who is going to go too the White House and overturn the United States Supreme Court Rulings. such as {Roe vs Wade.} and stop the senseless slaughter of Millions. They Do have Rights! Wait! Your one, that says there is no Life there. Well where is there? What is the Topic at Hand? Life! The Growth, That Became the Controversial Topic of the Conversation. Life! (clearly the High Court ruled in error or for agenda purposes?)

A Nation that would deny Life. That worrys' me greatly and a People, that have no understanding or appreciation of the precisious gift of Life, very troublesome. United States Court Decisions that have either inadvertently or possibly even obvertly established legal precedent or Judicial Rule, over it's Peoples thru "Healthy Fear" Policies and Strategies then being formated to, imitate "Supreme Authority or Creator Authority" as being established so clearly stated with-in the Constitution of The United States of America and it's Bill of Rights.

Replacement Theology of the Legal Kind; remove God from the "equation" and replace Him with goverment instead. The" Healthy Fear" polocies, that influence the Our Nations young children, generate a base of "FEAR" of the goverment it self with-in the public. Instead of having the goverment afraid of it's People with "Healthy Fear" in mind. strictly of course as a Managerial fear. The goverment would have us afraid of them. (Tyranny awakened?)

U.S.Supreme Court rulings that mirror the decisions of the German Supreme Court Rulings that eventually led too the Holocaust of World War 2. (I guess if we don't actually see the Holocaust it is'nt happening.)

A lack of "Real" leader-ship, A nation that has become so corrupted and polluted with so many of the Special Interest Groups and Forces continuosly pulling and chipping away at the very "Nature" of Our Once Great Nation. Sure, We are still militarliy strong. But, We have become a Nation that We do not truely want to be. and that is when Leadership has to Steer for the Good of the People. it happens to actually be mandated in law and spirit, when one swears to uphold the Constitution of the United States of America. (Where is Checks and Balances?)

Today, Our leaders display at times brutt force. Which directs the nation down a path of insanity and at the same time, attempting to sway public opinion as a "wiser man" or it was hard. But, I did it for the Nation or better still Humanity. However, the policys that are often created are almost always negative at best as well as being just widely unpopular. Seeming to go against the very grain of Our Society and Our History itself.(Change) and then they would have us believe that it was true leadership and not just political manuvering. (For the good of the nation) hu'?

I Trust God for my Health. The Lord Gives and The Lord Takes Away!

No "Man" or system can guarantee you your Life. Health care is not a right! Tell that too God The Best Insurance in the World can't Save Your Life! if you accept the idea that goverment can give you your rights. You better get ready for the goverment to deny you your Rights.

Insurance isn't the problem it's your Outlook upon Life! Who do you Trust!

Some persons may have come to appreciate" finacially appreciate" the benefits under the numerous Health Care Agencys. and at other times economical and physical streessing upon the sick and establishing in experience, if they or you or I had not obtained Insurance before hand. they, or we., would have had to possibly spend a large sum of money for medicines and medical procedures and visits with-in the medical community and quiet possibly, may have even lost ones health all together. and yet, some Insurance carriers have been said to have been prohibted to serve in some of the states. (created shortage. not to mention possible violations of the Constitutions Commerce's Clause?)

Theres certainly enough fear in the Country to motivate one to constantly fear life itself. Is it merely coincidence that every other television commercial seems to be another pharmaceutical company's advertisement. That has "Death" as a possible side effect. or the constant., class action law "suits" that are being currently pursude against the very thing you just ate for Breakfast or the Item that you just wore or touched at one time or another, in your life. Campaign of Fear? Ask yourself this, would it be in Your interest as a Pharmaceutical Manufacturer to create such deadly compounds and offer them too the Public. at the same time having to list all of the deadly side effects and other possible life threatening factors. of taking their products.(You might bleed out, But your sneezing will stop) Certainly not! You are I, would go bankrupt or worse, too prison for manslaughter or even murder. Thousands of commercials, who's paying for them? man created catastrophe? I would definately terminate my chemists and hire a morraly based advertising agency. (Healthy Fear?)

I find it puzzeling myself, How a Nation that promotes abortion as a "Right" can now suggest that they actually care about your Health Care. (Where Have You Been?.)

Were, you really surprised! When We go down that road theres no turning back!

The arguement has been made "Politically InCorrect" not debateable! What President has ever promised to attempt to influence the Supreme Court as needed? None! He can not, unless the very rare opportunity arises. (Presidential "appointments" in time of need alone.)Haven't all past Presidents claimed to be Christians even though the Proggressive Society would have persons accept the seperation arguement as fact, However, past Presidents have had to comply with the "social norms" for at least a while. until, Society has been so succesfully steered down the wrong path and seldom down the right path. (Alabama or Auburn) or (Democrat or Republican) or a Leader who will do the right thing.

The U.S.Supreme Court has been acting as the German Supreme Court of the Nazi Party! Truely! During those Horrible days of Adolf Hitler. (It was actually legal to exterminate the People under German Supreme Court Rule of Law.) However, The Laws did not hold water in the Court of the "World" during the war trials at Nurembourg. The very same Court. Where some of the very same laws and legal presumptions or legal precendents created under Nazi rule where now overturned and tried themselves. (Our own atmosphere at home; Tuskeegee Syphalis experiment 1932-1972, and of course the building blocks of "planned parenthood" being laid down in the early twenties, (they were a roaring!) Hypocrisy/Conspiracy? it would be sad for me, if I was just fabricating this stuff. unfortunately true, however.

The Founders of this Country would truly not recongnize us today. and we are told that the Constitution of the United States is a "Living Document" (meaning, subject to growth and of course change.) Will it to., be aborted? and you thought Enron was bad. you thought Bernie Maddof was bad. the never ending aquisition of wealth. resulting in larger White Collar and or Capitalistic crimes affecting the nation and other nations as well. (MADD?)

What about a Goverment? can it become just another common" dishonest" company? Is it possible? Is the System broken and what isn't broken is then just utilized to merely maintain power for the greedy and corrupt and we then are merely cattle grazing in the field. and then someone is thining the herd?

We have spent billions on space exploration (You thought the Ocean was vast when your ship capsized.) and we have been told that scientist as a matter of academic fact, will indeed discover life in space. However, if those same scientist discovered just one human discarded fetus on mars it would be proclaimed as the discovery of a life time and then paraded around in the faces of Christians and ignorantly proclaimed to be of course an even greater inteligence than man. They then would classify the New life form as being our alleged ansestors from Mars.

And I do not make or take these claims lightly. I base my understanding on years of research and experience and understanding of the History of our Nation and the" interpretations" of the Reading of the Law., it's almost as though we were all in the Dark Ages again, and the Roman

Catholic Church was reading the" WORD" for you. and telling you, the layman that you could not possibly hope to understand. Being a layman alone. Very similiar to todays lawyers and courts that interpret law and read the law for you and you need their all knowing eye and understanding of law, too see and ear to hear. (What would the Framers Think?)

That would definetly be a strange monster for the Founding Fathers to understand, I think that they would even want off the "bus ". It is not suppose to be this way.

We the Nation definetly got the "change" we did not want. and thats really scarry. that is, if the forces actually think that the Nation is willing to now sacrifice it's very Freedoms for a lolly pop and a imunization injection. and not to forget all of the Television Commercials that are constantly warning you of the potential ailments that you probably have or may have, if you have ever taken this medication or that medication and check with your Doctor. and not to leave out all of the potential law suits that you may be eligable to participate in and potentionaly sue some of those very same type of Terrible Pharmaceutical Companies. (Odd) Recently, The Advertising for these very same drugs has increased tremendously! almost as though, the 'pump of fear' were being primed with the social "collective perception" in mind. (Dont let a good tragedy go to waste especially if it's created?) What will history say.

The United States of America was established with Judaic/Christian beliefs in mind at the time as with it being the "Social Norm" and yet. That has become "politically correct". The Founders of The Decleration of Independence would roll over in their graves individualy, if they could and give you a place to park your "communist bycycle". or an about face of shame. (as military custom would diciate) We abort children like we abort marriages. A simple matter of convience. We simply can't afford another mouth to feed! We teach our children that they are possibly decendants from the apes. When? was the last time you saw that ever happen? I'll answer, never! We are now establishing the concept of same sex unions through the Country and likening the struggle with a legitimate struggle of the Historical African American. and If, I was an African American I think I would be a little angry! But, as for me. I have a little Native American Indian in my blood. When was the last time you heard of a Potential Presidential Candidate refering to them? The

Country is basically runing like this, "and I love to use analogies" this one really fits I think.

("There's a wagon train on the move and theres a whole lot of wagons with familys' following the lead wagon. In which, sit two men. Wagon Masters., it's their job to carry the settlers heading west in safety. However, They are fighting over control of the reins for some reason and the wagon train is now following so close, so not to be left behind, due to all of the trail dust from the trail in their eyes. That they are now Blazing a Trail West! A Land Train! Blindly following that rear end of that lead wagon. Now, just off too the side in the high Desert, stand alone, Native American Indians watching the progressive or hurried wagon train of settlers, unfortunately heading straight for the Grand Canyons edge. The Indians are actually saying to each other, "Somebody should do something, don't they see where they are going?" But, Back in the lead wagon. The two men are still fighting over the reins trying to seize power Not ever looking where they were leading the wagon train. and the settlers were following in foolishness never questioning their leadership. until, it was to late.

Here are some interpretations from Our Nations Courts and the Rulings that are well documented in the "Public Record" and as with all things today. Such as the Constitution, the Decleration and of all things the Greatest Book ever written The Bible are now a matter of "interpretation or perception".

Interpretations ie., What did the Constitution say about property or slavery? What does the Constitution say about Religion or Liberty? What is the Definition of sex?

Legal Rule of Law. what does the Court say. what precedents are created or established through the Supreme Court Interpretations of law? A Judicial Bench making law instead for the people instead of the people making goverment make the law by the people.

Here are a few of the United States' legal moments in time, that have changed the course and nature of being an American citizen of the romantic past, too the changing present.

(and still growing)

{1811—The People verses Ruggle}

The Supreme Court ruled against a Charles Ruggle for using blasphemous profanity, in which they, the Court ruled was a direct attack on the foundation of the United States of America, He was sentenced to three months in jail and fined five-hundred dollars. "five-hundred dollars, you do the math that would have been alot of money at the time, several years worth of hard earned salary no doubt.

{1953-Brown verses the State}

Here it would seem as though the Supreme Court litteraly banned the Bible from the public goverment school system and is said to have stated that the scripture would be counter productive and psychologicaly harmful too children and that they may just start believing in it again. was this the ruling?

{1958—Baer verses Kalmorgan}

Here it would seem as though the Supreme Court would rule that there is no finding of a seperation of "Church and State" and futher-more people should stop saying that there is, or people will soon believe contrary. was that the ruling?

{1973—Roe verses Wade}

Here it would seem as though under the "guise" of quiet possibly having denied someone their Constitutional rights. the court decided to hear the plaintiffs arguement and denied the rights of the baby., and the father., instead. But, mainly the Baby's Rights. (I guess if We do not see the Holucaust it is'nt happening.) was there a different outcome?

"When is it o.k. to give the keys of life and death to a single gender, thats what they did. Theoretically speaking, what happens when all the women in the world decide not to have anymore children. That would be the end of Human Civilization as we know it.

Whats going on in America,?

The American people have been indoctrinated "down". How? ask your self this. Whom, controls that little white school house on the top of the hill? It was public at one time, being that it was obtained through community need. Today it's gone federal, industrialized even. massed produced as desired on command seeing that one's indoctrinational academic materials are set in place steering society's children down what ever desired path as an educator would be so inclined and supported by the system to do. What are they teaching todays children then?

Doctor Benjamin Rush, a Signer of the Decleration of Independence and the said founder of five of the major University's Whom, was also known as the spiritual founder of our public educational system., stated that, "The teachings of Christianity must be in our Educational system for our form of Goverment to work." wise words still the same.

The Founding "Fathers" of America wanted to "assure" all later generations to come, That the newly created Goverment would and could work. Because, the People would govern them selves. How? The Gospel of Christ would keep the People on the right path. (Seperation of Church and State arguements do not cut it. just read the writing's of John Jay; Our Nation's first Supreme Court Chief Justice.)

Look at us today, the Decleration of Independence and The Bible have become two of the most mis-understood and manipulated writings ever. The Founders (of America) had it right in the begining, it was a Nation for All Peoples. Peoples of all races and creeds faught for this Country in the begining, They to faught against oppression and tyranny side by side., They established a Nation that even the Signers of the Decleration were recorded as saying that it must have been an act of

God and or Providence. Today, look at us. America's children are being indoctrinated down, making them and future generations now, dependent and vunerable to undesirable influences and eventually remaking society thru new social norms. They or we are fortunately blameless for some of these things, being that they are inherited with-in goverment. However, The Bible states, that the way you bring up a child is the way that child will go. So who's bringing up your child? Who are you allowing to teach your children? A Country full of latch key children. Parents that are found to be so busy chasing the "Hollow" American dream. A new dream, Not the dream of the Creator nor the nations founders. but the dream of the "Oppressor" So, who is raising Our Children? The State, with all the tools of reverse psychology at it's disposal. easily positioned to re-define our basic definitions and simple understandings of natural life and the orders of the Universe itself.

Goverment never intended for the Supreme Court to have so much power, It was intended to be a Court System for those that just didn't get the lower Courts decisions and or worst case senarios. It was suppose to be a collective base of Judicial Power to regulate and if need be carry out enforcement of the Peoples Will. Specifically., the Constitutuions Legal Authority. What happend there? Ever do any reading on the Trail of Tears? Whom, Democratic President Andrew Jackson deliberately and malictiously defiled the direct ruling of a once honorable Supreme Court. Can you imagine being a Cherokee / Christian in the dead of winter, or of course other Native American Indians tribes alike with a new born, a sick wife or child and then systematically being death marched. Sounds alot like the Imperial Japaneses' bruttal forced death march of thousands of prisoners of war too BATTAN, during World War Two.

(The stage is set, just cleaned house, I guess cotton producers can fill the lands of the south now in safety. an economic experiment can now begin and the goverment loves experiments)

CHAPTER TWENTY-TWO

DIVISION

The Civil War, what happened there? We are often instructed in Public or even Private Schools that Our Nations unfortunate and costly Civil War was mainly inspired by the South s' un-quenchable apetite for "cheap labor", which was true. However, it seems a little to dishonest to just reduce the tragic historical events into sound bites. (Political Manuevering)

It seems as though a general blanket of deception has been spread upon our nation and key important details are occassionly left out through accident are direct acts or actions of persons re-writing our history.(a general dumbing down of the masses if you will,) It's true that the Southern States by consenses; Were "Democrat" and not "Republican" and heavily re-lied upon the pro-slavery rights They professed exsisted which enabled" them "too finacially prosper. However, if "One" in the South today, is confronted by the imperical evidences of this fact, They most likely tend to grow hostel are even resentful are even angry. Declaring themselves as not a pro-slavery morone; that is to say, They never personally owned Slaves or never would do such a terrible thing. However, the reality of the topic has been twisted and altered to accomodate current political parties, Abraham Lincoln was a Republican and not a Democrat, "irony?" (Why or How could the first African American President choose the Democratic Party then?) Andrew Jackson was a Democrat and he seemed to have ruled with an iron fist.

When President Abraham Lincoln took office, He and the Republican Party had ran on the anti-slavery ticket or political platform. and State after State succeeded from the Union fearing the loss of it's presumed States' slave-holding resources and again their presumed rights. it was the Republican Party that looked to Free a People from the un-godly nature of slavery, The President Himself encountered resistance with-in his own Pro-Slavery Union and it's military establishment of order. and even Some Northern States and even the City of New York is said to have desired an allegiance with the pro-slavery south.

President Abraham Lincoln's image is on the U.S. Treasury Bank note, or I.O.U. as a five dollar amount of value and yet President Andrew Jackson is on a twenty. Why is this? and why do American Native Indians have a built in dislike for Jackson? "The Trail of Tears" Andrew Jackson defied the Supreme Court Ruling in Worchester verses Georgia in 1832 and continued without restraint and continued cruelly removing Indians from the South and their native lands. (pre-Civil War South) and in doing so. He (President Jackson) opened the fertile grounds of the Southern States to Farmers and imigrants alike. (just as the western frontiersman being allowed to migrate west into Indian territories, a bad idea, but one that could and would be explotited later by the Federal Goverment.) and in doing so., the Southern states grew.

Twenty or so years later the Nations Civil War would be just about ready to begin. a nation divided by whom? President Abraham Lincoln took to the Nations Office and had a Nation being divided by finacial gains and immoral human behaviors. The Republican Party had won the Presidential election running on the anti-slavery platform. attempting to correct a wrong by those "legal eagles" whom suggested that slavery was protected under the Constitutions' property clause. when in fact there is no clause that gives a person the right to own or inslave another.(what is the defintion of sex?) Abraham Lincoln seems to have taken an Office when no one really wanted the responsibility of doing what was right.

However, just as the sign on the inside of the commercial plane that clearly states., Do not open in flight. some idiot did just that. The Constitution was amended when it did not need to be amended with the thirteenth and fourteenth amendments. The U.S.Constitution does not grant anyone the right to keep or own slaves period. but "Legal Eagles" who seem to make a living subverting our own Constitution may have manuevered thru loop holes of "what is the definition of sex?" or in this case property. and State after State succeded. (Blood in Blood Out?)

It seems as if someone has been attempting to dumb us down, Why is that? Personally, I have my thoughts on this and due to the fact that I am writing this short little book, I am able to spend as much time as I like explaining, if you will only indulge me. I'm a Christian and when I feel or sense a dumbing down attack, I always reflect upon My Greatest of ancestors Adam and Eve. They too were dumbed down by clever conversation from the Father of all lies, Satan. A very intelligent creation that no man will ever match wits or I.Q's with. Adam and Eve were pretty smart and still were convinced into thinking that it may just be possible that they did not hear GOD correctly, when HE said; "The day you eat of that fruit you shalt surely die" Today we can read this account and I hope that you do or will, and say to our-selves ; How could they have heard something different? or maybe just maybe if we forget what we as the "enlightened" now understand the action of free-will that GOD allowed to occur and look as un-educated or un-enlightened without understanding and take it for face value or on the chin if you will and use our imagination or reason, one must see that manipulation with-in conversation is a very dangerous platform. (To be continued) ★   ★   ★

(The Union Army can invade the south and destroy lives under the premise that they were liberating the black man. but, what was the true intent and outcome of the civil war? "Federalism" or a Monopoly on Power?)

During World War 1, the policy of the federal goverment was that a black man couldn't be a capable soldier. as they confined the black man to trivial and minimal duties.

During World War 2 the Federal policy was pretty much the same, Desegregation. but during this War public attention was focused probably in letter format adressed to so many of our respected congressmen. Wondering why they, the African American can not be officers and soldiers of all diciplines, just as the cocassion soldiers. And then we have growing desent in the ranks of the population taking the format of correspondences, public protest and just your average "American Citizen voicing their Voice". The goverment seems to have figured that it has to throw America a bone,. So it conducts an experiment. "The Tuskeegee Pilots", and where better to place it than in the State of Alabama. If it fails, you could just blame it on the South, They are racist and the North isn't. (yea right!)

The Goverment may have never intended for the experiment to actually work. Location location and location. It is said in some circles that it may have had to have taken a visit from First Lady, Elanor Rosevelt whom was visiting the Airbase and had to insist on riding with one of

the new pilots. "DON'T LET A GOOD TRAGEDY GO TO WAIST."
I am not a racist by any means. But I can clearly see the work of liars and
evil men all around me. Persons taking advantage of circumstances and
innocent ignorance and sometimes even creating events. as I believe has
occured in this Country from time too time.

A younger generation will come to remember the Tuskeegee Airman,
Because of a movie or rather and just possibly a new generation will be
distracted from the real story.

The Tuskeegee Syphilis experiment, conducted in the State of
Alabama from the year 1932 too the year 1972,. I recently asked a friend
how could He could now trust a goverment in regard to his health care.
When the same said goverment was capable of doing such evil things as
the nazis', and willfully infecting so many persons with such a horiffiying
and deadly disease as syphilis. His reply, What are you talking about? (He
had never even heard of such an experiment.) I wonder how many other
people have never heard of the experiment conducted by the" Federal
Goverment ". President Clinton has. Remember Him apologizing on
National Television? I guess He had to re-assure the American public
that we can actually trust "them." After all, He did apologize. and yet,
He., had no stake in it. or did He? or They?

Ever hear of the Georgia Guidestones? Again, I had not heard, until
recently myself, and boy was I surprised. Right there under our very
noses this entire time and it's just white washed over by the media, or
not reported at all. Makes me wonder whats going on in this Country.
If your not a Bible believing person, a child of the most High God, You
better start believing now!, its a good idea.

This Gigantic "Privately" Commisioned monument stands in the
Beautiful state of Georgia and if your not familiar with it, look it up.
and if you cannot, Let me share with you a little about it. It's a huge
multi-monlithic stlye monument standing in a field which simply states
in eight different languages. The World should reduce it's total population
down to 500.000.000 people and have no more, and additionally have
a One World Order and One World Relegion. It's located in the State
of Georgia. sure! put it, right in the "Bible Belt." irony., if you will look
into it you will also see that it happens to lay with-in the same general
rotation of The Apple of God's Eye. just a coincidence I'm sure.

(Satan standing upon the Earth shaking his fist at God) saying "Look
at them Now!"

Do You watch the History channel anymore? It's amazing that all of the years the so called inteligent scientist have spent and spend attempting to spread the doctrine and belief of evolution and the idea of a creator such as the creator of heaven being a weak mans religion. and now they discovered that we are the supposed aliens and that GOD himself is an alien. Do they hear the words coming out of their mouths? They, I believe hope and wish greatly that the American people have been dumbed down so much, that they may have some eating right out of their hands. (We live, in truly dangerous times surrounded by dangerous minds!) The Bible says that they will start worshiping creation rather than the Creator. does that sound familiar?

Why, are so many people then so mis-informed? We have the internet, We have the telephone, We have library's full of books and no one reads them. We claim to be a connected society and yet persons can't communicate, In the Bible it also says that it will be like in the Days of Noah in the end of the last season. "God likes gardening by the way", have you ever wondered what does that mean? Does it mean that GOD will flood the Earth again? No. He said he would never flood the Earth again., but if you listen to the Global Warming so called Experts it remains a possibility due to the supposedly melting polar ice caps. ever hear of Magellon? What was it like in the days of Noah? Well there were mockers and scoffers. there were really evil peoples, that was one reason "GOD" had to flood the Earth, to save humanity from itself. What put mankind in danger of it self to begin with? ever read Genesis? ever hear about the tree of what? Knowledge of Good and Evil. Mankind ate of that tree and man-kind had a duty to be the chief of his house, Thats why women have had their positions in life, they were tempted first and gave to the man. but GOD knew she would, HE planned for this to happen so that his own Heavenly Will would take form," free will". GOD wants children, He could have just created us from the begining to be His Children and never go through any of this, But what would" He" have created., children that were made to love Him and not children who instead choose to love Him. Who was jealous? The brightest angel of them all, often called the angel of light. What was it like in the days of Noah? The days of Noah were the direct result of the fall of man and the fallen ones, are they still here? demanding no continuing their assault upon GOD? You bet. and we are the prize,(If the Prince of Darkness can have GOD'S desired children mocking and murdering and acting like a bunch of idiots, that would make him very happy I'm sure.) Nimrod the "Hunter of Men" may also be a part of the" equation" of Noah, pre-flood and past-flood. The Descendants of Noah were there to relay the story of the World Wide Flood and God's Judgement. Nimrod did what? He gathered workers and constructed a Gigantic Tower with the ambition of reaching into the Heavens,. The Bible tells us that God saw the works of the Descendants of Man, knew their Hearts and destroyed the Tower of Babel and forever changed our tongues and colors so as to disrupt the collaboration of "evil man". (Sound Familiar?)

CHAPTER TWENTY-THREE

PARTIES

Who do I vote for? Am I a Republican or am I a Democrat?

The answer is neither. Im a Christian, and voting in the Country has unfortunately become an event likened unto buying a raffle ticket in "Soddom and Gommorrah" merely hoping for the lesser of the two evils. and the "Political Partys" seem not to care about doing whats right! They feed off the emotion and fear of the People. If you will study Our own history. They play against the American people inciting mob anger and inspiring liberal thinking which aids in the attacks against the Constitution it self.

Should we be angry and call for the "Goverment" to take over all Banking and Private Buisnesses. Because of corrupt practices and policies that favored the Banking Systems profit marigins were the cause of the "Housing Market" or instead, Shouldn't we be more angry with the goverment for inadvertantly or advertantly orchestrating the finacial catastrophe to begin with. (Wisdom) The American dream being defined by banking and supported by Goverment polocy. Someone else's dream again. Why American? If it's America's dream the system then needs to start teaching children How to solve their Housing needs and get out of the "Socialist" way of collective thinking and truly educate children for the future. Who's future?

The "Frontiersman spirit" were did it go?

There was a time not to long ago, when a "citizen" could actually mail order an actual "mail order house" and the "House "was designed and assembled and then un-assembled and literally shipped to the customer. The Customer would re-assemble their new home and provide a dwelling for their family. Others had the ability and knowledge to carve out their "Homes" in the Wilderness and the "Homes" became villages and communities and the Nation grew and stretched it's borders.

Where is that Common Knowledge and Know How, today? We have spent decades now re-molding social norms. For instance, How many citizen actually know how to build their own homes? even a bird knows how to build a nest and a spider it's web., In the "Cowboy days" not too long ago; before the plane, before the automobile, peoples who had not the technologies that society has today. Were, Still able to obtain homeownership. Is it dumbing down or advancement to be in debt for a "Dwelling", to be held prisoner if you will; homeowners having to rely upon those that would possibly take advantage of the home owners ignorance, in regard to cost and or repairs and we all know that thermo dynamics will effect all things material. (Take out a reverse mortgage now!)

So then everyone needs a Home. ask yourself this, What is your or our school systems viewpoints and or rather the "Goverments" perspective on Home ownership in America? what or how are they preparing a future generation to prepare for this human goal of material aquisition? We can put man on the moon, we teach our kids how to be soldiers before college and they may even get college credit for training now. but., we can't break away from the goods and services teachings. and teach them to build things themselves. to be more independent. and certainly one can see all around us the over all influence upon society. resulting in the crushing of the human spirit and the reforming of mans nature. Which influences growth and physiology for all humans in association with the Industrial age and the alterations from Invention. ie. an automobile means less walking. which may contribute to someones health problems. and many other examples can be easily suggested.

They seem not to care or have their duck's in a row at all. (or perhaps they do?) we do not teach our children how or why they should learn to be self reliant, "we" the system instead stress the need of conformity and acceptance of someone else's "dream" and where you or they must look and apply themselves so not to rock the "boat" and fit it in.

Goverment has taken on the huge responsibility of leveling the educational field and attempting to place all citizens on the same economic plain, however, what has been achieved, other than mere indoctrination into the" Ways of the World." (are you too, surrendering your commission for all that glitters?) by making bricks.

The Housing and Banking collapse, homes under water, people loosing their homes because of dis-honest and un-wise banking programs that were generated and proped up by the goverment itself.and now we are suppose to be angry with the "banking system" and would need futher intervention from the "Goverment" the same goverment that helped to create the problem to begin with. (Don't let a good tragedy go to waiste?)or create one if at all possible.(Fannie and Freddie)

What are they teaching the "American" children then? Debt is good. We measure a persons worth by the established "credit score" system, if a person pays cash for a said item and not instead assumes a payment of debt for said item. We or the system actually punishes the person by lowering a persons "credit score", as if to imply that a "citizen" who does not support the idea of managed debt is somehow un-american or even finacially incompetent. Since when, is going into debt common sense. (irony, When one considers our Nations debt and the lack of a Balanced Budget.) The Constitution clearly states that Congress has the right to tax the people in order to" pay debts". The line of thinking then and apparently now must have changed drastically since then. They, the Founders of the Nation thought apparently on paying their debts unlike those in goverment today.

They spend and spend and suggest that if there was a Balanced Budget Amendment it would stop. It is easier to spend someone elses' money. The need for a Balanced Budget should be common sense. It has already been addressed with-in the Constitution, already. For members of congress to suggest a Balanced Budget Amendment is to abolish and insult your common understanding of the Constitution altogether. (Here we go again, with whats the definition of sex? mentality) as with the Thirteenth and Fourteenth Amendments, that in my opinion should have never had to be written in the first place. Since the Constitution never restricted anyone in particular other than the Native American Indians. Persons have "read-into" the original writings and have subverted it's original intent. and because it isn't actually in the Constitution, Legal Eagles subverted the basic premise for the understanding of "property" (sound familiar?) and insisted on rights alleged under the Constitution and saught to finacially prosper. President Abraham Lincoln had to close a liberal leaning "open window" of doubt. with the amendments directly addressing the isue of slavery. since the word slave or slavery does not exsist in the Constitution to begin with. (Criminal minds will seek windows of opportunity)but that is a different book.

Most Presidents in my opinion are just the same as all of the others, in my opinion. in the desire to manipulate the Constitution and Our Bill of Rights. "It seems to always be the agenda". We Declared our Independence from England and stood on the top of the World, and said we were a Christian Nation out loud! Don't you think that the Evil of man heard? and said oh' really. We'll see about that. and now look at us, the Country is more of a Bible believing "nation "than is presented or now reflected with-in the" Mass Media and Entertament Arenas" and most importantly Our Public School Systems and Goverment Institutions. and still, People are afraid to speak the truth for fear of retaliation. From who? The Goverment and the mob mentality. (Healthy Fear Policy?)

The First Amendment states among many other important decrees, that goverment will not make or show any favortism toward a specific denomination or belief. However, what then is the theory of evolution? is it not a religion? it certainly is not science. As a Christian I can often find myself attempting to explain my faith and justifying my beliefs. and still as an educated person I realize that interpretation is in the eye of the holder or for arguements sake, the scientific mind. It then becomes a stance of faith. or interpretation. (theres that word again)

Evolutionist believe in things not seen but instead theorized alone. and they are still searching for the missing link which would support their theory. A question of faith established on rocks. rather than a religion based on the Creator of rocks. (Jesus told Peter when Peter confessed Jesus's Heavenly identity, on this rock I shall build my Church.) and now., we are worshiping rocks. So then, why wouldn't the Theory of Evolution which has still not been proven as fact. not be considered as a form of religion? Why then, is the goverment thru it's public educational systems influencing or honoring a particular religion. Academic censorship?

The very" censorship" the founding fathers of this Country attempted to prevent in the first place. Freedom of Speech. But we never seem to see what the left hand does or see what the right hand is doing? or did. We should, But with the Hollywood distractions and television mentalities today, People just seem not too care! ("convenietly distracted") I speak out loud and voice my growing dissonance and people tell me. I am to passionet and I should take a little blue pill, and stop worrying so much.

and yet, I constantly observe them worry over stupid trivial things that do not even matter. The American people have dropped the ball and all We need to ask now is., When will it be our time to get onto the train?

Ever stop and think, How could Germany during World War Two do such a terrible thing?

How could so many persons be so apparently evil. Where they? How could a German police officer who was typically a person interested in fighting crime, or a German Soldier and citizen as well, just tell the Jewish people to keep the "Peace" and get on the train. What was going through his mind, What type of person was He? A Thug, an Indoctrinated Brown Shirt. or just an indoctrinated citizen. Whom was influenced by political powers and the German Supreme Court which also being influenced became the mediator between Dictator and the People, creating the "problem" to begin with. and what about the Victims? Why would they just obey and willingly travel to their death? (Healthy Fear Policy!)

They allowed "Replacements" of all the Persons not Loyal to the Nazi Party and merely kept the image of "Authority and Law" Sound Familiar? (See the Trials at Nuremberg) Adolf Hitler was freely elected in a Democratic Society. and still, When our own History refers to his administration it is often convenientaly left out that He (Adolf Hitler) was elected in a Democratic fashion., It is always convenietly left out. and its always suggested as being just the "Nazi" form of goverment. Adolf Hitler came to power through stirring up the mob mentality. Once elected, He too, used "Presidential Powers" to make all of his political "replacements" through-out the Goverment of Germany; persons that were bullies and deviants, people that would enjoy power and never question the leadership. a newly re-educated type of German citizen, who, were recieving pumped up propaganda through none other than the German School system and the National Media. (Sound Familiar) Do you want a "mob of citizens" who will favor your method of insanity? Well educate them or at least indoctrinate them as with the use of special interest groups. Thats what Germany did. As Americans we can certainly say that we can see these same types of influences everyday, or at least on the television and certainly with-in the School systems., which has become a tool of the "special interest groups", and their influential powers., I was once a person who watched television quiet regularly or so until the last Presidential election. and I observed People electing a man that America didn't even know a thing about. and Where? were the so called "journalist" who could have expelled my reluctance. (Honest Journalism is dead?)

How can 95% of the Media just push a single" candidate" without ever doing their job! Where's that old college journalistic couriosity? They went to school didn't they? How deep does the conspiracy go? President J. Carter, whom during His administration did his part in weakening the Sovergnty of the Nation. Whom, also became a one time sitting President and had appeared to have dropped off the face of the map. Until, literally returning from the wood work to go on too National Television and tell the American people., That if you don't agree with President Barrack Oboma, it's because you are a racist and he can easily make the claim with his vast knowledge of our racist-views in the South. Excuse me Mr President. But, that was the most irresponsible statement that a person could make. Much less, the Former President of the United States of America! and wheres the story there? Why didn't anyone do an in depth report of this strange television moment?

If the corrupt powers are not using the television they are using the school system, President Bill Clinton during his Administration created the "must carry law"., which states that for every hour of religous programing there must also be an hour of balancing programing, what does this mean, exactly? I was watching television just recently and came across a channel that I found very disturbing, a pornoghraphic channel, right away I was even being enticed, wow! look at that, just right there in front of your eyes,. I wondered for a moment how easy it has become to become an immoral person in America. now I'm not knocking sex, But, it is best kept between a man and his wife. We have one of the highest divorce rates in the world. We have prisons over flowing with sex offenders,. We have aborted over an estimated fifty-million children. now that's more than Hitler was able to murder, and the sad reality of making so many young women victims and unknowing accomplices whom will have a serious conflict of acknowledging blame or guilt, will this help create a mob mentality? one of many surely, almost as though giving ones' neighbor strong drink and dulling their senses to take advantage of them and rob them.

Everyday in America a little girl goes missing and it's usually a sex crime oriented event or occurence, committed usually by an already sexual convicted rapist. yea!, must carry law, huh?

Will this be good for Society and "Legal precedence"? My own Mother recently came across several channels a short time ago and became very disturbed! She imediately thought that someone in Her house had been watching "dirty" movies. So, She picked up the phone like any Good Mother would do and called Her satelite provider to complain, and She was told that they could not merely block the programing due to "freedom of speach issues,". Remember Larry Flynn? actions are taking place in our Nations Court Sytems and laws are being changed and the people are ignorant to the same It's as if the Goverment passes a New law, waits a period of time, doesn't fully express the implications of the new "political measure" and then tells us that it's been on the books for a while and due to lack of funding they were not able to enforce the new measure, "pass and delay". Pass it. Then we can read it! Thats exactly what the last Speaker of the House, Nancy Pelosi said, in reference to the Socialized Health care system shoved down our throats. (I watched Her say it.) and thats also a matter of public record.

So, let me get this straight, the Government would have us now believe in little green men, by proxy, and possible "evolutionary agenda standards," If you believe you still came from a rock! The Goverment commited mass murder of the native American Indians and experimented on them as well. The Goverment removed the Bible from the public school system because they were concerned about your childs mental devlopment, and did not want them to believe in the Creator, "Well that alone is treason" The goverment allows women to commit mass murder and at the same time becoming victims themselves through Their Un-educated choices, which are a direct response to political planning and special interest groups. The goverment experimented on the people of Macon, Alabama. infecting them with Syphilis for God sakes!

The Goverment merely slapped Tobacco Giant Philip/Morris on the hand when whistle blowers reported the evil deeds of the company. "To big to fail I guess", and now, We are suppose to believe that the Goverment actually cares about Our health.

Polotics, during the "Gulf War" we as a Nation and member of the United Nations. responded to Suddam Husseins invasion of Kuwait for profit. after he, had exhausted His Nations' Treasurey during the fight between Iran and Iraq. As the Leading United Nation power the United States invaded Iraq to protect the interest of the State of Kuwait and in doing so found itself acting as Global Police Force again as in the Korean War and the Vietnam War. However, more like unto the Korean War in that there was no clear victor and a stalemate insued, with a demilitarezied zone and no fly zone clearly established.

Iraq became the next North Korea and soon became isolated due to it's aggressive and murderous form of rule. Generals and Soldiers alike did not seem to understand why the United Nations stopped it's pursuit of Suddam Husseins ambitions. (Confusion?)

Inconvienent for Iraq that the Goverment of The United States would then enter under the premise of War. after having recieved a deadly attack on 9-11. Terrorist hijacked civilian planes and declared war on America. unfortunately for us they died on that day. and could not detail the terror network. We would have to wait for confirmation from the network itself. As the suprise attack on Pearl Harbor many had their lives cut short by War. But unlike World War 2 or the Korean War or the Vientnam War, Our enemies do not wear uniforms.

Instead of the Nation viewing the assault as a criminal affair. We were reminded of Pearl Harbor instead and began an invasion of the middle east. with Suddam Hussein convientely in the cross-airs. creating a no win situation all around, you can't possibly hope to occupy the area for ever. Futhermore, when Our troops invaded Iraq they made more enemies than were initially there. it would be common sense to make this conclusion.

We, as a Peoples for instance commited open rebellion for Our Freedom and faught bravely against King George the Third of England.

But we were not there to build nations, we were and are there to iraticate extremist. apparently where ever we find them. (Russia had their Vietnam in Afganastain) and now we are continuing the War on Terrorism as if it were a Tangeble thing or idea. and not understanding your enemy is a grevious tatical mistake.

The War on Terrorism has certainly outlasted the War of the Worlds. and will continue to exsist as long as there are differences among peoples, Muslim extremist primarily and now secular humanists and even possibly atheist (if the mob meantality convinces them of the need to remove all percieved henderances to their imaginations of space exploration, seeing that there would be a need for funding to accomplish getting lost in space.)

Saddam Hussein gassed nearly Five-Hundred thousand Kurds, fearing an up-rising against his insane regime which may have resulted in his ousting. (WHERE DID HE GET THE GAS?) We allowed Hussein to remain in power as type of" Foreign Checks and Balances" against a yet more and possibly more tyrranical Country, Iran.

Iraq and Iran have been at war for years and we and our Nations State Department used Suddam Hussein as a means of again "proxy" defensive line strategy. until the war between those Countrys left Iraq finacially broke, resulting in the Nation of Iraq unfortunately and with no real forsight launching an invasion into Kuwait to seize monitary and physical gain.

The United Nations invaded Iraq under the premise of securing the State nation of Kuwait and protecting the peoples from evil. However, after invading and pushing Hussein back into his on Country we seem to have stopped the assault and created yet another North Korea/ South Korea. unfortunately for Suddam Hussein 9-11 would be over the horizon.

A war or enemy of convienence? A modern day Pearl Harbor just happened. although there are tremendous differences in Japan's attack and Muslim Extremist. and we have had a past experience with Iraq as the English lossing Singapore to the Imperialist Japanese, so boots on the ground! Invade somewhere? It's interesting how the liberal media seemed to bash then President Bush for looking for weapons of mass-destruction and suggesting that there were none at all, as if they actually represented Iraq themselves. Which brings to my mind. Do they not know that military gas is a weapon of mass destruction and even more importantly is, where did the original gas come from? The United States equiping Suddam to fight Iran? maybe or just probably may have done just that.

A war with no desirable outcome on the Horizon and a People confused by the "Fog of War" allowing a Goverment to obtain more power over its' people under the guise of security for our future as a nation. (Healthy Fear by Proxy?) an attack on the foundation of the Spiritual History from with-in as with so many controversial court rulings can be more destructive than an act of terrorism.

Instead it would have been better for the Nation to have allowed the Federal Bureau of Investigations to do their job. (it was an act of crimminal behaviors) being well equipped for any matter of criminal investigation. and instead, the Nation is carried to WAR. and then terminologies that are being created in an effort to understand or label the enemy are also finding themselves being used to describe all religious mentalities even with in the Judaic/Christian Faiths. and thats very dangerous, remember Waco, Texas. and the Branch Dividians.

Most people would believe that all of the parties (Branch Davidians) involved with-in the sad affair were all tried and convicted for murder or armed sedition or just being "extremist". However, they were not convicted of crimes and instead those that perpetrated the actions of the Policing were found to be in violation of the Branch Dividians' civil liberties.

CHAPTER TWENTY-FOUR

WRITING HOME

I wrote a letter too the Governor of my State recently attempting to give a new Governor a chance or the opportunity to be made aware of my situation, The letter reads as this. and with all mispelling just the same.

"Dear Sir, My name is . . . . I am writing too you due to the overwhelming conditions in regard to my life, I enlisted into the State National Guard during the time of October of 1986. to hopefully become a member of the Special Forces."

I originally desired to serve with-in the regular Army, but after having my ASVAB score lowered by a Military Recruiter which caught the attention of a First Sergeant by the way who questioned the lower Sergeant as to why and how?

I decided to listen instead to him being the higher ranking non-commissioned officer. He suggested that I speak with someone else, while the entire time his subordinate was attempting in my opinion, to change his mind.

I entered into the Special Forces recruiters office and was imediately asked, if I had pencilled in my new score? I replied, no sir, the Army recruiter had done so. His reply, we don't do that!

I stated that because I had been thought of as an under-cover police-officer at my new school, my guidance counsellor, who also thought I was a cop, suggested that I could recieve my General Educational Diploma and simply graduate earlier,

That same G.E.D. was used to grade me on "The Curve", as the regular army recruiter had put it. and yet the "Green Beret "recruiter said we don't do that!

I enlisted into the Alabama National Guard with the hope of going full time.

During basic training at Fort Jackson, South Carolina, I was the perfect soldier, always squared away, a true leader and someone whom Our Nation could use.

During training I was assaulted by Drill Sergeants other than my own, on several several occassions and where offenses occured witnesses watched and came to my defense.

I was almost shot, doubled gassed, physically assaulted and told that the G.E.D. that I was kicked out of Public High School for, and the said same document which was used to lower my ASVAB score, no longer exsisted!

So now, I have two G.E.D.s, the numerous and unbelievable events in basic training alone are far to many to list. "I think it would make a good book".

I continued on with my training, occassionaly having N.C.O.'s ask me if I. If I was C.I.A., why would they ask a private this question, but they would just say never mind private.

I finally found myself training with the Marine Recon and the U.S. Navy Seals', by the way doing the very thing I was told that I wasn't capable of doing.

After all of my training my classmates recieved their orders and left, I was National Guard and yet was stuck in Fort Lee, Virginia. for months without orders.

One day, I was called to report to a Colonels office, for what? I do not know, I remember sitting in a huge chair, directly across from the Colonels desk with a Major kneeling down whispering in my ear, (what? I do not know)

I remember the Colonel telling the Major that he doesn't know anything.(referring too me)

The next thing I remember is standing on a sidewalk, at a phone booth with the reciever in my hand, I suddenly "came too" and said helo'. But no one was there and no change fell out when I hung up the phone. suffering "flu like symptoms" I walked back to my assigned barracks looking for a familiar face, only to realize they were all gone.

After at least three months of my actions or memory un-accounted for and the sudden feeling that I was "awol". I started walking toward my barracks, to be met by a Senior Drill Sergeant whom slung open the main doors right on time as if he was waiting on me. to tell me that my orders had been cut. I do not even remember how I got back home.

Ironically the first thing I remember when I came too in the phone booth, was that I was AWOL. I returned back to the state of Alabama and literally went AWOL. under a since of distress! Who was I going to tell this ordeal too? I wasn't weak, I wasn't a slacker, I was the better soldier at all times, but I just returned home to a unit that I didn't even know and they didn't know me.

I was actually allowed to just leave," Hell" I maybe even missing for all who are concerned are interested with-in regard to my very expensive training and service contract. I would welcome the Military Police in my driveway.

I wrote Senators of Alabama and attempted to contact military lawyers and they only respond with, So, what do you want me to do about it!

Im now contemplating seeking help from the American Center of Law and Justice and God forbid the A.C.L.U., but would rather communicate with the newly elected commander in chief of the Alabama National Guard.

Are you familiar with Major Frank Camper of Dolomite, Alabama, he was apparently training real mercenaries and I apparently was placd in the net with him.

I t's the only thing that I could have done or been alleged to have done and that would be untrue or a mistake, I enlisted into the service or at least attempted too serve with a desire to do at least twenty years, retire at a young age and then continue working for the Goverment.

I would love to speak with you in person if possible, their are far to many details to include in this letter.

P.S. I've written a book, but Im not an extorter, If I have my day in court, I would own the military and the agency.

Yours Sincerly,

. . . . (actuall leter)

I recieved a return letter from the Govenors Office shortly after, it states.

> "Dear Mr. . . . . . : Thank you for taking the time to contact my office regarding problems with the Alabama National Guard.
>
> I have directed your concerns to Major General so in so, Adjutant General of the Alabama National Guard. I am confident that the General and his staff will evaluate your request and take appropriate action. Should you have additional comments, please contact General so in so at (000)000-0000.
>
> Thank you again for sharing your concerns with me. If I can ever be of assistance to you in the future, please do not hesitate to contact my office again.
>
> The Governor.

"This is an actuall reply to my letter, there seems to be a little disconnect between the citizens and those that are our elected leaders.

I have yet to recieve assistance, and I never had a problem with the Alabama National Guard, they were not there!" The right hand never see's what the left hand is doing apparently".

So in closing allow me if I may, to attempt to summaraize the elements in this strange equation I have unfortunately found myself in. I thru coincidence alone, happened to have been a friend of a friend, whom's father happened to be working with the "Goverment" under cover. and working under the premise of being a Mercenary for hire in an attempt to actually protect the United States and it's Allies. and I became assimilated into a series of events in which I took no part in, nor had knowledge of or gave support too. However, the "Agent" whom operated behind the cover as being a mercenary was somehow, himself, lost in the shuffle and found himself imprisoned for a duration of time. at the time of His mis-fortune I was having my own mis-fortune while attempting to serve my country. At the same time being under suspession of being a trained mercenary. (Timing is so important.)and while, I was being treated as the un-wanted step child and dumped upon the street. The agent was being exonerated and the event would be white washed with-in the media. However, it would seem possible due to the nature of the events. that the goverment would continue with it's activities. Which would explain why so many officials through out the System would wonder if I was a member of the Agency itself. For what other reason could a Drill-Instructor ask a kid in basic training if he was C.I.A.? or, a law enforcement officer asking the same thing several years latter, or the fact of being "awol" for so long and no one seems to care. ask yourself. Who does that. Who do they think I work for? them or some other agency. It may just show us how our own goverment operates in the big "casino of scemes and themes". (Dont get lost in the shuffle number one.) Well as the circumstances presented themselves, I was forced to step back and observe my nation truly for the first time. The forced pause, if you will, allowed me to see things truly for the first time. God works in mysterious ways indeed. Seeing how, I desired so much to serve my country in the capacity I pursued and if it was up to me. I would have been a blind soldier following the blind. Instead, I have been able to see and experience things that others have not and some still ignorant of the same. (Our Country is Broken.)

(When Israel was still young and found itself surounded by neighboring Kings they desired to have a King of their own. Israel asked the prohpets for a King. They wanted a King as the other surrounding empires had and God then, warned them of the dangers associated with having a KIng and told them of the troubles that would fall upon them because of a King. But still Israel wanted a King. God gave them Saul.)

This simple pearl of wisdom was well known by the Founding Fathers of this Country being that they were more Biblicaly Educated, unlike today. Logic would then dicate that this basic understanding derived was the main idea of a small goverment, principal. You really don't want a King other than Christ.

There are solutions but thats a different book.

Do you know see why I have never voted? "Was it Ben Franklin or Thomas Jefferson who once said that all it takes for tyranny to thrive is for good men to do nothing"?, Wait it was Edmund Burke the man accredited with being the philosophical founder of Conservatism that used that expression. (Edmund Burke 1729-1797.) Well it's "flaunted" in Our faces daily. The powers that be, mock you! with the heavily manipulated elections and the reeducational programing of the Media and general television programming telling you how to think or what Yours or My opinions should be based on the created and televised

"Social Norms ". Do you actually believe that the most powerfull Nation in the World would really or could merely allow some some unknown person to assume power? Its a scam America, it isn't what it was suppose to be! Did you vote for all of this to happen? All of the past "Commanders in chief" of this Nation. since, my conception have all claimed to be Christians. Do you really believe that they were? I am a Christian. and I would fire every person in our Goverment and our Nations Founding Fathers would roll over in their graves if they could and salute me! and if they were true Christians do you think they would have honestly made so many controversial appointments to the Supreme Court. or initiated so many un-christian minded policys.

We do more of an in-depth' background check on potential police-officers than we do on those who will be telling our officers what they, will be doing. (i.e, polygraph examinations, maybe a new version of How many marbles are in the jar?) There is no correct answer, they did not want you to have the ability to serve ones on Country and that is the real tragedy., Why? Are some to Honest or to Patriotic? If We desired to have any potential Presidential Nominee administered the same polygraph test as a Potential Police-officer, it would be said to be politically motivated. (Polygraph test do not work!) if they did, All crimes would be solved. All International and Foreign Policies would change, we would all know everything, what stock to purchase, what mechanic to trust, which employee will protect your Companies interest, which potential maritial mate will not commit adultery and so on.

My Dad as always stressed to me the importance of doing things right. If your going to do something do it good and give all that you have.

Recently, I noticed a Church sign that said. "You may be the only Bible that People get a chance to read." I was perplexed for a moment and then realized how true that actually is. As believers of the Word it is Our duty our Great Commission, to spread the Truth of God's Word. Do not be afraid of the mockers, the doubters and those that think "relegion" is a weak mans hope.

Jesus warns us that in the end, their will be terrible mentalities, mockers and blasphemors alike. (But, We should remember that we too, may have been these very same people at one time or another in our own journey thru life. So we must be wise as serpants and gentle as doves.)

Heres a thought for you, I often wondered why was Jesus assisted in carrying His cross, was He weak? but He was a carpenter, aren't carpenters always carrying wood? why was He in need of help? and then, it dawned upon me. Jesus was beaten so bad, before He was crucified that all other humans would have surely had died before being crucified. Man is He tuff! He walked through the streets under great strain, like no one else, He stumbled, He fell, I wonder how many times He fell, was it seven? He carried the cross and could have made it if He wanted too the entire way, but He didn't,. He allowed another to pick up His cross and help Him, and that was a strange gift to the church or the "bride" pick up your cross and follow me! they hated me before they hated you.

"PICK UP! YOUR CROSS".